REBEL

WITHOUT APPLAUSE

PATRICIA PANERO SHERR

ISBN: 978-1-98-300764-4

First published though Opus Self-Publishing Services
Located at:
Politics and Prose Bookstore
5015 Connecticut Ave. NW
Washington, D.C. 20008
www.politics-prose.com / / (202) 364-1919

Contents

PART I

PART II

PART III

Rebel without Applause

Why Write A Memoir?

I have lived a long life and kept friends from childhood onward, regardless of moving constantly all over this country and traveling the world. Several of them have encouraged me to write about it. According to them, my life has been unique. I always have a funny story or two to tell from different times. Childhood, teenage years, marriage and a fascinating career make up the vignettes shared.

I grew up in an affluent exurban family. As a girl, I was expected to do nothing. That was easily mastered.

As a debutante in New York City, even I knew how vacuous we were as a group. Our vague goals: find a husband, raise a few children, know how to entertain and maybe have some knowledge of the Arts. Oh, and also, do a bit of volunteer work e.g. join the Junior League.

Living near New York Hospital, I applied to work there as volunteer. For some reason, they sent me to Payne Whitney – one of the best psychiatric wards on the East Coast. Many famous people suffering from "nervous exhaustion" made up the patient roster.

Then I met and married a concert pianist, who captured my heart with his music and his good looks. Life changed drastically when I became the principal bread winner.

By accident, I developed into an expert at opening hotels. Working for Four Seasons, Hyatt, Westin, Loews and other groups took me to many interesting places to recruit and staff 18 different properties. They ranged from 200-2000 rooms.

This memoir then is something of a thank you note to my family and friends, who have so enriched my life. It is a series of short stories covering different stages of my existence. It could be considered a "Coming of Age" memoir, except I'm still growing up.

My Parents

My father, Guy Panero, came to this country as a teenager in 1905. Born in Piedmont, Italy in 1892, he was the youngest of four children separated from them in age by at least 10 years.

Family lore says that his architect father, Secondo, was a political rabble rouser who came to the United States to escape the tumultuous situation in Italy. Two children were already here: Amelia, an opera singer and Mario, an engineer.

He attended Stuyvesant High School in New York City. Money was scarce. He paid his way through night school at Brooklyn Polytechnic Institute. He worked as a draftsman where he gained knowledge "on the board" while studying mechanical engineering. He enrolled in graduate studies at Columbia University and City College and became licensed in 1924 in New York. Two years later Hegeman-Harris Builders hired him as the Chief of their Mechanical Department.

For these builders, his early projects included Rockefeller Center, The New York and the Chicago Daily News buildings. Then the company sent him to Europe where as Chief Engineer he participated in the construction of the American Embassies in London and Paris, the US Pavilion for the Paris Exposition of 1937, and Earl's Court Exhibition Hall in London.

With all this traveling, each of us children were born in different places: Bob in Chicago, Arthur in New York, and I in France. All this time my father remained an Italian citizen. When Mr. Harris left Hegeman and formed his own company,

J. W. Harris, my father joined him.

As WWII approached, we returned to the United States living in the New York City area. My father was involved in the 1939 World's Fair construction. Through the depression era, he was fully employed. His skills were appreciated; particularly, his ease in dealing with disparate groups of people.

My father eventually left the Harris firm to join H.K. Ferguson company to manage engineering projects in the defense areas located primarily in the South. He became a U. S. citizen in 1942. While working for Ferguson during the war years, we lived in Louisiana, Tennessee, Mississippi and Ohio. When Mr. Ferguson died, my father assisted his widow and took over management responsibilities.

At the end of the World War II, the US government sent my father with other scientists and engineers to study the chemical processes in Germany. At the same time, he studied their underground installations. When he returned to the United States, he worked with the Defense Department to see if those types of facilities could be duplicated in this country.

At the end of the War, my father bought a fading engineering company and built it into an international organization, Guy B. Panero, Engineers.

Besides being located in New York City, he established offices in Paris and Rome to manage joint ventures for the construction of universities in Tehran and Bagdad. Other European projects also developed. The company became successful nationally and internationally.

His alliances and joint ventures kept him engaged and traveling constantly until the last year of his life, when his health began to fail. He was 69 years old and had undiagnosed hemochromatosis: a disease that deposits too much iron in various organs of the body. If diagnosed early, the cure is simple and old fashioned - bleeding. Today, this disease is easily treated. He died in 1961.

My mother, Anna McCormick, was the daughter of James McCormick, an Irishman born in Belfast, Ireland. He became a New York Policeman. Her mother's family, the Bennetts, had been born and lived in Brooklyn for many years. She, her three sisters and a brother were raised in the traditions of the Catholic church and fierce loyalty to Ireland.

It is a mystery to me how she and my father met and married. It might have started in the workplace. Her family and probably his, did not approve of the idea. How they survived their nationalistic preferences to marry, is anyone's guess. The topic never came up for discussion in front of me.

All good looking, my mother and her sisters had lively personalities and vivid blue eyes. That gene is so strong that virtually all their grandchildren have them.

My Mother was about 5' 4" with a curvy figure, slim hips and the great legs of all the McCormick girls. She was outgoing and friendly, sang, played the piano, and was generally adventurous and resourceful.

They married in October 1927. Within that year on an assignment, they moved to the Chicago area. My father's firm kept him busy and traveling constantly. My mother who had lived in one place all her life, spent the first 10 years of marriage moving constantly: Chicago, New York, Paris and London.

Douglaston – Early Memories

Born at the American Hospital in Neuilly, France, a suburb outside Paris, I joined my two brothers, Arthur and Bob, five and seven years older. Paris before WWII, even with the shadow of impending conflicts, created wonderful memories of a magical city for my parents. At that time, my father acted as the project engineer for the American Embassy. From France we went to England where he directed more projects.

Although my father had come to America as a young man, he still retained his Italian citizenship. During most of the depression years he worked in Europe. Those years brought him success and a solid reputation. He was brilliant, skilled and tri-lingual with a certain style that had lured my mother away from Brooklyn and her Irish roots.

In Europe as the chance of war seemed inevitable, the family returned to the United States. We moved to Douglaston, Long Island, a small village near New York City. This is where my earliest memories begin. It was and is a charming town on the water, an easy commute to Manhattan.

My parents travelled often and my maternal aunt Honey became my main caregiver.

My memories are blurred but I recall a fire in the house, and how Honey roused me gently out of bed. There was no panic. I'm not sure where we went, maybe to her home.

Later, I heard some stories of the fire, but mostly how grateful my parents were that the firemen had saved two or three baby pictures. No one mentioned lost possessions.

In a later memory, I recall walking with Daisy my Nanny, and Sally, my best friend. Maybe we were three or four years old. Sally had five siblings. She and I formed a bond that has lasted many years through marriages, divorces, deaths, our grown children and grandchildren.

There was no lack of money. My mother managed the household and entertained family, friends and business associates constantly. Add that to the scene with my two lively brothers and me, there were few dull moments.

My father never lacked self-confidence. He was bright, energetic and capable. He seemed to understand how to deal with people at any level, as did my mother. Of all things learned at home, it was that skill.

As World War II began, we moved to Baton Rouge, Louisiana, then Jackson, Tennessee and later Tupelo, Mississippi. My father became an American citizen in 1942. The US Government needed him for the War effort. I remember little about each place.

However, in Baton Rouge I remember a Christmas Eve Mass when my father, who rarely went to church, fell asleep during the sermon. Mother nudged him, he woke suddenly, loudly snorted and went right back to sleep. My two older brothers and I just laughed out loud. Mother blushed bright red at our antics. We were always hard to control, but that was the limit. Dad was never asked to church again.

My other memory is being chased around our big back yard in Baton Rouge by my brother Bob on his pony. Also, I recall how upset I became to learn from my brothers that there was no Santa Claus. It was just Daddy. From day one, the two of them probably wanted me gone from the household. The five and seven-year age difference between us loomed large. It meant that as the baby, a lot of love and attention came my way. There were times when I was sure their goal was to kill or maim me.

They never had a chance. My mother probably saved my life with her vigilance.

The Patsy

People ask me to tell them more about growing up with two older brothers. I didn't live through their early years, but did hear stories.

My mother told me that they were impossible to deal with. Both as young adults and later in life, they were smart and energetic. As little kids and later on, they skied, rode horses, played tennis and baseball, and golfed. They were constantly on the move. Since I was born in Paris, Bob, my oldest brother ended up speaking fluent French. My mother managed to see that he retained the language permanently. Arthur, not as outgoing as Bob, never did have much to say anyway.

Arthur was easygoing and not quite as lively. My guess is the boys controlled the household. Their world revolved around their athletic activities and social life. Mother when widowed, admitted to me that she never was able to manage them, which is why she introduced them to sports early in their lives.

Bob was more than intelligent and definitely a leader. Even as a young boy he had the ability to influence his surroundings. During World War II was the only time we were all together in the same parochial school in Jackson, Tennessee. I, in first grade, Bob in 7th and Arthur in 5th.

One time, there was a school contest to collect wire hangers for the War effort. Bob called Arthur and me to a meeting. He said: "Patsy's little, so we'll take her around the neighborhood to ask for the hangers. No one will say 'no' to her. We'll follow to see that she doesn't get lost or in case anyone gives us hangers on the spot. Together, there's no way we can lose."

He pointed out that the grand prize was a huge box of candy. Bob was right about everything. No one ever said "no" to me.

My most vivid memory is of one of the mothers telling me,

"Stand in the driveway. I'll go up and throw down a bunch of hangers from the upstairs window."

I stood in the driveway of the enormous house and hangers rained down on me. This type of event happened often. On a daily basis for two weeks, people showered me with wire hangers. We did indeed win the contest and a large box of chocolates and other candies, all rationed during the War. Mother Superior handed me the prize with Bob at my side. He had lifted me up on stage.

"Here, I'll hold that for you."

We accepted congratulations from our classmates. Bob said to them:

"See me later, we'll share some of the candy."

Apparently, he ate a candy bar or two and sold them on the school's black market. I never had even one bite and have no remembrance of Arthur's participation in operation "Hanger." Bob deftly led his small team and we gladly followed.

In his high school years, Bob went to Kentucky Military Academy. Not surprising that he earned the nickname, "The General." Totally, take-charge person, he could, if necessary, herd cats and charm the grumpiest dragons. I wonder if my parents needed some time away from him.

Whenever he returned for the holidays, his little troop fell in line for any new bright ideas for possible mayhem. He was to his dying day a lot of fun to be around.

Summer in West Hampton

In 1945, we began to spend summers in the Hamptons. We rented houses big enough for lots of friends, family and parties. We joined the Country and the Swim clubs. Both of my brothers looked older than their ages and loved women. The women returned the feelings. Bob, slight of build with dark hair and vivid blue eyes had enormous self-confidence and charm. Arthur, tall, broad shouldered with black hair, navy-blue eyes, was movie-star good looking. With the difference in age, I could only observe them from afar. Also by now, they didn't physically threaten me, although they reminded me of my ugliness on a regular basis.

I was indeed pudgy with a face full of freckles. Kids would ask me if I had measles, or say things like "what happened to your face." Worse yet, I had absolutely no athletic ability or inclination. I took tennis and swimming lessons, but never won a game much less a set. Swimming was better, at least I knew how to stay afloat.

Being shy making friends was hard. Mother rarely let me out of her sight when I was little and still kept the reins tight. (Probably saving me from the wrath of my brothers.)

I did have my friend Sally, who came and visited every summer. She usually spent most of the vacation with us. Our parents were long-time friends. She, unlike me was tall, slender, beautiful and a good swimmer. All the boys liked her, but oddly enough I wasn't jealous. I was happy to have her company and could trade off a bit on her popularity.

West Hampton was a small quiet town in those days. We rented a big house next to a Polo pony ranch. The owner was friendly and glad to have my brothers exercise his horses regularly. As a result, neither did any chores related to the house.

There was a broad expanse of lawn in front of our rambling two-story house with a driveway in the rear. As the summer wore on, the grass grew greener and taller. By August, it came up to my shoulders but then I was not particularly big. My most vivid memory is of my father in his custom made Italian suit, his silk tie askew, standing on the front steps. He was annoyed to see the grass so high and harassed my brothers for never mowing the lawn.

"I want it done today!"

Bob's answer, "We're just too busy."

Arthur, "It'll take forever!"

Dad, ever the problem solver said: "Fine, then just make a path through to the road."

He never wasted time in useless argument.

Boarding School

At the end of the War we moved to Forest Hills Gardens, close to New York City. After years of constant travel my mother decided that unlike my brothers, I should go to only one high school. This meant boarding school.

I started at the Convent of the Sacred Heart in Greenwich, Connecticut. I never had to finish grammar school. My grades were excellent and there were just a few months left to finish before the September start date. With an A+ average, no one thought anything about me skipping the last half of eighth grade.

The first year turned into a disaster. The teaching at the parochial school lacked the rigor of the Convent. The Sacred Heart nuns were a teaching order and could not take vows until completing college. Part of their tradition was to pursue advanced degrees and many had doctorates. A great deal was expected of us. My parochial school teachers had not been too well educated, nor were they in any way demanding.

To add to the problem, I was shy from the constant moving and traveling. My family offered great security and closeness. My classmates were on the whole sophisticated and quite rich. The new environment required a major adjustment. For the first time I had to study just to make a passing grade. Also, our daily life was regimented. Students rose early every morning to attend Mass. I did not thrive. We were away Monday through Friday and home on weekends, which was a small break in the routine.

Initially, my mother drove me to Connecticut every Monday morning and usually picked me up on Friday. Sometimes I shared rides with other students from the Forest Hills or Kew Gardens area.

I hated to miss my favorite Monday night radio program. It featured a baritone, Gordon MacRae singing operetta and show tunes in the company of various talented sopranos.

Sometimes, after arriving at school I would play sick, wanting to return home to listen to that particular show. After a day, I miraculously recovered and Mother took me back to Connecticut. Those first two years, I looked pretty healthy but had a reputation for being somewhat sickly.

Because of my constant complaints, the short sick days and the 2-3 times a week my mother drove the New York to Connecticut roads, my parents decided to move to Greenwich. I could switch to the Day school and live at home. Looking back, I was definitely spoiled.

The move to Greenwich worked miracles for me. Several friendships blossomed. I learned to drive and when I got my license, my parents gave me an old car.

The company my father acquired came with a 1944 custom made 4-door Cadillac convertible with automatic drive. It had been sitting in storage and now was mine.

The first time I drove it out of the driveway to practice on our deserted back road, was almost my last time behind the wheel. To turn around and go home I pulled into a driveway, slowly backed out and quietly hit a large tree. The left fender looked bad. My mother watching from the front door, looked furious.

A few days later driving with the top down, I waved at a friend and side swiped another car. My parents gave me one more chance. After that, I decided to become an extremely careful driver.

Connecticut in The 1950s

Motivated by the fact that I hated boarding school, we made our move to Greenwich, Connecticut in 1950. The goal to see me graduate after 4 years at the same high school remained important. After 2 years of boarding school at the Convent of the Sacred Heart, I became a day pupil. It changed me.

We went from apartment living to a gracious big house on the water.

We always had domestic help and I learned from them. I understood that whoever served us in anyway, deserved respect. One of them Lee, taught me an interesting lesson. One day in chatting she made the remark. "You know all you white people are the same color." I didn't respond to that statement, but realized I thought all black people were the same color. My eyes were opened permanently. From then on I looked more carefully at both black and white people.

I learned to listen to and observe the society around me. My intuition served me well. Because as a family we entertained frequently, I met and talked to a wide variety of people. This background served me well in life and in business.

Radio Show Audition

One of only a hundred girls enrolled in this high-priced Catholic High School, the nuns singled me out for my singing voice. They convinced my parents to have a coach come weekly from New York City to train me classically. My teacher, a tenor, sang regularly in Opera and Concert performances. I loved to sing but best of all I loved to miss sports.

The only drawback occurred when I realized the school expected me to lead sing Georgian chants. Intoning the Latin prayers in all the cherished rites every morning became a way of life. It can be hard to talk at 7:00 a.m. much less sing. However, I always reminded myself how glad I was to have field hockey forever off my schedule.

When the Glee Club performed, I usually sang a solo line in the lyric range. My clear, high notes carried easily over the chorus. No one outside the choir, knew who was singing. The nuns wanted me to remain humble. While the chorus performed standing on several layers of risers, I stood on the floor hidden behind them. One notable song "The Prayer of a Norwegian Child" so moved one of my classmates, that she wept. She told me afterwards, "It sounded like an angel singing." That comment amazed me. I just opened my mouth and sang out without much thought.

I wanted to sing popular as well as classical music and decided to look for a radio job. One afternoon, I walked into WSTC a local station in Stamford, maybe ten miles away from home and asked to see the manager. The offices were not overly intimidating and the receptionist was friendly.

Mr. Schwartz, the manager came out to see me.

"How can I help you?"

"Well, I'm looking for a job."

"What kind of job?"

"Anything, sweeping floors...anything."

When I look back, he must have been chuckling inside. There's no way I didn't look like a local rich kid.

"What do you really want to do?"

"Sing: maybe have a radio show."

"OK. Why don't you find an accompanist and come back for an audition? How about next week?"

More than a little stunned, I agreed. I left him and called my friend Rachel, whose father always played for me. Mr. Vuono agreed immediately and we set up the date.

Mr. Vuono and I appeared at the studio at the appointed time. When we walked in, Mr. Schwartz and Mr. Vuono were astonished to see each other. They had been high school buddies. Here's how the audition went:

"Can she sing?"

"Oh, yes, it's lovely."

I never had to open my mouth.

Mr. Schwartz gave me a 15-minute segment on Saturday nights. That particular station's radius was perhaps 25 miles.

To put together the program, I showed up at the studio on Wednesday evenings. The only friend I trusted with my secret, drove me the few miles to Stamford each week. I shared no information with my family.

The station had a musical library of popular songs. I put on earphones, the music piped in and I sang along. I concocted a little script and called the program "Melody Lane with Pat Panero."

Listening to the program on Saturday nights presented a challenge. The station's radius was miniscule. To locate the program, I set the library clock radio to tune into that station at precisely 8 p.m. My family knew nothing about it.

One Saturday evening several guests were visiting, sipping cocktails on the porch overlooking the water. They were preparing to go out to dinner but the evening's conversation delayed them. I, in the library reading, had forgotten to watch the time. Then: "This is Melody Lane with Pat Panero" and my voice singing out "I've got you under my skin, I've got you deep in the heart of me." The radio program came on and music filled the air.

I heard my parents outside: "What's going on? Does Pat have an orchestra in the library?"

They found me turning off the radio and stopped me. Thoroughly embarrassed, I explained about the program. They thought it was great.

"Why on Earth didn't you tell us?"

"I didn't want the nuns to find out."

The result: In the interest of the nuns' desire that I remain humble, I quit.

Looking back at my life in general, I loved singing but not the limelight.

Flying Down South

During one Easter vacation, mother and Aunt Honey wanted to spend a week in Pinehurst, North Carolina. My tiny mother planned to drive her huge Cadillac in the company of my even tinier aunt, from Connecticut to North Carolina. I did not want to spend all that time watching scenery fly by. Being a typical, rebellious teenager, I refused to go unless I could fly. Mother was scared of planes but agreed since she was more scared to leave me home alone.

Flying out of the small airport in Westchester County into Charlotte, I missed my connection to Pinehurst. I had no cash with me since according to my parents, I was "too irresponsible to handle money." My only asset was an expensive sapphire ring and a certain amount of naive confidence. This was years before credit cards or cell phones were in the hands of teenagers.

I figured that maybe I could take a flying lesson from the airport flight school and use it to get to Pinehurst. I let the owner-instructor know that I had no money but could leave my ring as collateral, retrieve it and pay him on my way back. For some reason he agreed. He said no to the ring, but yes to the flying instruction. We flew his twin engine Beechcraft into the rustic Pinehurst landing strip. In the air he let me take the controls for a while. He showed me how to bank, turn and watch the instruments while he pointed out landmarks. It was an informative trip.

When we got to Pinehurst, a taxi took me to the hotel, where the room clerks welcomed me and paid off the cab. After checking in and unpacking, I headed for the stables. Mother and Honey hadn't arrived yet but were on their way. Who would leave this 15-year old alone for too long?

I found a riding instructor who took me on a trail ride for an hour and then into the Equestrian circle where he gave me a lesson in show jumping. Finally, riding my horse back to the hotel, I saw mother standing on the veranda, hands on her hips and an angry look on her face. She was livid. "Wait until I tell your father, you are SO irresponsible!"

She took me up to the suite and put a call through to Dad. She went on and on about me hiring a plane, hiring a cab, hiring a horse and just charging it all to her. As she tried to impress him with my bad behavior, I could hear his laughter through the phone.

She gave up and handed me the receiver. His response: "My god, you're resourceful, but please try not to spoil your mother's vacation, okay?"

They never did seem to agree on child raising techniques and/or discipline.

First Trip to Europe

One summer, my high school offered a chance to go to Europe with the Institute for International Education. Then it was a small organization willing to taking a group of Catholic girls on a six-week tour of Ireland, England, Holland and France.

It was presented as a competition but looking back, if you had enough money and were not a troublemaker you would be chosen. I was ecstatic to be included in the trip. A few other schoolmates also joined the group. We sailed on a small ocean liner that had two classes instead of the usual three. Our group had ten people. Three or four girls from other schools joined us as well. Our ages ranged from 16 to 21. Two charming older women chaperoned us. They were both intelligent, very nice and well connected wherever we landed.

Our shipmates were friendly and had some interest in us. Looking back at the pictures, we were an attractive assortment of young girls. For me, it was my first time on a major trip without family.

The ship landed in Cork, Southern Ireland. Our chaperones had friends and contacts there who entertained and welcomed us. We spent several days in Dublin and then headed for England. I, and one my schoolmates, stayed with the Lewis family, old friends of my parents who lived just outside London. This was 1951 and London still showed signs of the War. The Lewis family welcomed me with great warmth considering their past friendship with my family. Also their daughter was marrying the son of other family friends, the Shireys.

Mr. Shirey headed the American Express Office in England. Between the two groups, we were often treated to dinner and taken on informative side trips apart from our regular traveling companions.

At some point in the trip, I decided that flying home would be more fun than another Atlantic crossing. On a whim, I went to American Express and asked to see Mr. Shirey. His secretary appeared and ushered me into his spacious office overlooking a busy London street. He sat behind a huge desk and rose when his secretary brought me in.

"How are you doing? Do you have a problem? "

"No, I just was wondering if you could talk my parents into letting me fly home...the boat trip is so long and boring. "

"Sure, I'll call your Dad. I'm sure we can work it out."

After a few days, my father called to tell me he'd talked to Mr. Shirey and arranged my flight home. He also mentioned that mother was upset and didn't want me flying anywhere. As mentioned she was deathly afraid of planes. Dad advised me that he knew I wasn't because I had been secretly taking flying lessons with my brother, Arthur. We would drive to the nearby tiny Westchester County airport for lessons, every few weeks. My mother had no idea.

Debutante Days

My first year at Manhattanville College in Purchase, New York, I was invited to "Come Out" at the Gotham Debutante Ball in New York City. The invitation went out to most of my classmates. The Convents of the Sacred Heart existed to educate upper class Catholic girls. It was their stated mission. So for a princely sum, we could be presented to Society, in this case, Cardinal Spellman. The money went to various Catholic charities. Not everyone accepted the invitation, perhaps half of those asked.

The debutante season ran from Thanksgiving to the first of the New Year. The most prestigious ball was the Grosvenor. The Gotham was strictly for young women from the best Catholic schools. The Galas usually took place at the Plaza and the Waldorf Astoria. The idea was to introduce us to society i.e.: the marriage market. A rule of thumb: if not married by 21 the latest, you faced the inevitable question: "Why isn't a nice girl like you married?"

I, for one, had not been "out" at all. Dates were few and far between. The best I could do was to give many parties and have many friends. My parents never objected to entertaining small or large gatherings as they preferred to have me safe at home.

For the Ball, you needed the proper gown and two escorts. I worried that no one would want to come with me. However, two of the nicest and best looking guys from the Greenwich neighborhood were glad to be my escorts. They were both over six feet tall, good looking and smart – one at Yale and one at Georgetown. Each came from local families and were fun company, besides being attractive.

Mother let my stunning sister-in-law Joan pick out a dress for me. She was a bona fide post-debutante. She was 5'8" with a natural sense of style. I was 5'2", and a bit plump. I enrolled in the Dubarry Success Course to lose weight. Let me only say, I failed. My slender and chic fashion expert picked a bouffant gown that would have looked perfect on her. On me, it looked okay, but looking back it emphasized my pudginess.

It had a full skirt, a pinched in waist (which to this day I don't have!) and too low a neckline. The obligatory waist cinchers popular in that era left me breathless and uncomfortable.

The Ball in November was held at the Plaza Hotel. Because we lived in Connecticut, my parents booked a suite for the night. When I arrived at the hotel and unpacked, my shoes were missing. Penny loafers do not work with a ball gown so mother lent me her shoes. They were a size too small but would have to do.

The debutantes stood in a receiving line greeting guests and then walked in procession with their fathers for the presentation to the Cardinal. He was a small man dressed in the traditional floor length red robes, with a red beanie covering his round head of limited hair. We wore net stoles to hide our necklines from his view. Our fathers led us to the stage, where Cardinal Spellman greeted each of us by extending his ring to be kissed. There was a lot of standing, posing, promenading, and acting dignified.

The fun began with dancing to the music of Lester Lanin. His repertoire of fox trots, waltzes, and even the Charleston contributed to the fun. After a while, my feet hurt so much, I gave up – stashed mother's shoes under some drapes and barefoot, danced away the long evening. Since I'm short, and my escorts were fairly tall, it often looked like they were dancing alone.

It was a night to remember. Totally entertaining. The only drawback: No one pursued me. I may have "come out" but went right back in January 2nd.

The Westport Playhouse

After we moved to New York City, my days were filled. I added acting classes to music lessons. This in the era of the Actors Studio, the Neighborhood Playhouse and Stella Adler, the actress and teacher who coached Marlon Brando to his success in theatre. The Broadway theatre thrived: "Streetcar named Desire", "The King and I", "My Fair Lady" were some of the hits of the day.

The last year living in Greenwich, I applied for an apprenticeship at the Westport Country Playhouse. The well-known Theatre Guild in New York City managed it. They accepted me into a group of about 12 people. We were unpaid and expected to do a great deal of physical work. We painted scenery, moved props on and off stage, cleaned bathrooms, and kept the rustic playhouse in perfect condition for the theatre goers. We were assigned to individual stage managers and expected to follow their orders to the letter.

I remember sweeping out the auditorium while watching "stars" of that era, like Imogene Coca and Eva Gabor rehearse. Christopher Plummer was there at the beginning of his career, appearing in a play "Home is the Hill" headed for Broadway. The play itself did not do well, but Plummer did. Leonard Bernstein presented one of his musicals "Trouble in Tahiti" for the first time. The theatre Summer Season often functioned as an "out of town" tryout.

When we were not working on a specific production, we maintained the theatre and dressing rooms, and waited on the visiting celebrities. We baby and pet-sat for the players. It was fun and I learned about "Life Upon the Wicked Stage" one of my favorite songs from the movie "Showboat."

One benefit: we always were invited to the parties hosted by Lawrence Langner and his wife Armina Marshall. These two people gave the Theatre Guild its strong reputation. Langner had formed the Theatre Guild in 1919. The Guild Board members shared responsibility for choice of plays, management and production. Over the course of years, they regularly produced hit Broadway shows like "Oklahoma" and "Porgy and Bess." When they branched out into radio and television, their attractions were then enjoyed from coast- to- coast.

At the parties in the Langners' country house, we apprentices mingled with the stars. That glitter alleviated some of the slave-like existence we signed up for. Most of the visiting actors were friendly and included us in their conversations and informal get-togethers. The setting in Westport was casual yet serious. We were not given acting classes as part of the deal, just exposure to talented and successful performers.

A group of us shared a small 4-bedroom house. My life until this summer had been sheltered. My roommate Edie, introduced me to a whole new world. Edie was in her 20's, from somewhere in the Midwest and had come to New York to find fame and fortune. This pretty, petite, outspoken blonde, with no prompting volunteered information on how she survived in the big city. She proudly showed me pictures where she posed for nude calendars.

"Most of my boyfriends give me any money I need. I love being in New York and being a model."

She seemed proud of her way of life and her ambitions. She wasn't at all embarrassed telling me her story. I was amazed and enlightened since I had never met anyone like her, or at least anyone who talked about it.

A more startling fact was that at age 19, I had never heard foul language of any kind.

In this environment, F....ing was the most prevalent adjective in use. S...T was also extremely popular. Every time someone burst forth with these expletives, I turned bright red. I'm fair and any blush took forever to fade. Then someone would start up again, and again I'd be red- faced. Being so totally unworldly in this setting called for drastic measures. One afternoon, I took time to lock myself in the house bathroom and staring into the mirror repeated every swear word over and over again until I was cured. It took about an hour of total concentration. The behavior modification worked: I just didn't know that was what you called it. I hated feeling so under-confident and plain dumb.

The entire experience was informative but the lack of privacy sent me home for a week. I realized that to survive in the theatre the inner toughness required was not natural to me. When selected to appear as an extra in one of the plays, I said no and pleaded illness.

The stage managers didn't like to have me assigned to them. With no self-confidence, shy and not used to the earthy people around me, I just clammed up and listened a lot. One of my friends Ellie, was a beautiful dark-eyed, dark haired, incredibly bright, young Jewish woman my age, with absolute self-confidence. I watched her create contacts and jobs for the future with ease. She knew how to cater and flatter people without over doing it. We ended up as life-long friends. She became a successful writer. She had grown up in an anti-Semitic community in Massachusetts and as a result, never cared or worried about what others thought of her.

I met and mingled with people foreign to my existence. Some of the players were open and instructive to us: others just used us as servants.

One young man, Frank Perry was working for the Guild and left it to produce the movie "David and Lisa." Anyone could see his determination, intelligence and drive.

The apprentices made up a varied group. Two of them were sons of a Hollywood actor, another the son of two famous producers, the father from Hollywood, the mother from Broadway. She came to visit us and helped launch the career of Tammy Grimes, then working in the box office. Christopher Plummer appeared in one show and those two found each other at least briefly. The other apprentices had strong ties to the film and theatre worlds. I turned out to be the only one with no contacts. I had written a letter, was interviewed and chosen. It was simply good luck.

The experience stayed with me as did several of the friendships. Some of them came about because of mutual curiosity. They wanted to understand where I came from, as much as I looked into their roots.

Curiosity has always been a major force in my life.

How Dilettantes Spend Their Time

Growing up, my parents did not want me to take a job from a person who needed it. Not allowed to work I filled my time studying music, volunteering and lunching with my equally idle friends. In general, we did nothing of much value. My only asset was I made friends easily and liked to help others.

Living on Sutton Place near New York Hospital, I applied, there as a volunteer. Initially, they sent me to work in the Emergency Ward. The first time they sent me out to the parking lot to retrieve a severed finger, I asked for a new assignment.

The head of volunteers said, "You'd be perfect for the Psychiatric Ward." They sent me to Payne Whitney – one of the best clinics on the East Coast. A roster of famous people suffering from "nervous exhaustion" made up the patient population. Every time a celebrity was reported to be in that condition, they were inevitably at Payne Whitney.

All I did was show up a few times a week, play bridge and chat with the patients. My assignments were on the 6th floor ward, where the patients were ambulatory and recovering. The objective was to help them adjust to going back into the community they left.

I learned to listen and be patient. No one was impressed with my bridge skills and once someone even threw his cards at me. But then maybe he had a point.

Some people would sit speechless and motionless in a corner. Others seemed as sane as anyone.

The uncomfortable part occurred in my social life. I would bump into their relatives, or them, after release. No one went there without coming from an affluent base. I lived in the New York world of Café Society as well as being part of the "Social" Scene. This included my contemporaries who like me could be classified as the "idle rich."

As a post-debutante, I participated in organizing charity balls. We were a vapid little group. One day when I showed up for a preliminary meeting, everyone was talking about a new addition to our committee.

"His name is John Logan. He's good looking, single and from a wealthy family. I think he's a Yale grad."

The chatter went on and on. Everyone was thrilled to have an eligible bachelor in our midst.

Stunned, I said nothing. I knew that within the week he would be permanently committed to a psychiatric hospital in Rockland County. He had just been diagnosed as a hopeless schizophrenic. That experience ended my "career" as a post debutante. Grow up time had arrived. Without telling anyone why, I dropped out of that scene permanently.

The lesson learned: choose your friends based on their character and intelligence, not on perceived social standing.

Dora

When we moved to New York City, Dora Davis McKinley became our maid. Now, you would call her a housekeeper or a nanny. Initially, she tended to the needs of our three-person family in New York City: my mother, father and me. My two brothers no longer lived at home. Then, as their children and mine came on the scene, Dora ended up taking care of all of them born between 1956-1963.

When she first started, she managed our immediate household in a seven-room apartment. Dora was probably 32, African-American, 5'3" with a lovely face, big brown eyes and a nice roundish figure. Her face glowed with warmth and intelligence. Her common sense was apparent in everything she did. She liked working in our home because no two days were ever the same. We lived at 50 Sutton Place, a large apartment building. My father's business was successful; we lived well and entertained often. Dora an excellent cook, and liked to be part of the numerous parties that my parents gave.

As my brothers and I married and children appeared, she began to fill in as an extraordinary caretaker of seven little people. She was the first person for whom my small son declared his love.

Dora awakened in me an interest in the entire concept of affirmative action. One day, when I was still quite young, she came to me and said: "Our only service elevator isn't working and they won't let me on the regular one. "This would mean she would be walking up and down more than seven flights of stairs, handling laundry at the same time.

Even though inexperienced, I knew no one would question me on the front elevators if I accompanied Dora on her trips back and forth to the laundry. Dora probably knew that too. I spent the afternoon with her on these chores. Our friendship began that day.

Dora created in me a quiet firebrand. I had been clueless about racism, until I saw her discriminated against in our building. I had never experienced or had the least idea of what poverty or want of any kind involved, much less racism. I had never been deprived of anything or experienced any type of discrimination.

The unfair treatment of Black people was everywhere I looked in "liberal" New York City. When I asked my parents to raise her salary as I thought it too low, their answer was that she could count on them if she needed money. Did Dora know that? Probably, not.

Once I went with Dora to her apartment in Harlem. She rented two large rooms, in a lovely old townhouse. She talked to me about how neighbors resented her attitude and found her "uppity." It might have been related to the high standards she demonstrated in almost every area of her life.

The apartment was immaculate, spacious with tasteful and comfortable furniture. Being curious, I wanted to know more about her life. One issue became clear: when paid weekly it was hard to accumulate money and she had no benefits of any kind. She educated me. She made me understand the obstacles she faced. I wanted to help her and others find ways to improve and expand their lives. It became my mission.

When I married, had a child and began working in the hotel business I was able to change Dora's life and that of her husband. She always had work, but he had more difficulty in finding a job. Because of my position as a Corporate Employment Supervisor, I found him a union job in a luxury hotel. Besides good pay, the benefits and the stability gave them a better, more secure existence. They were finally able to leave Harlem and make a life in the suburbs.

Because of my deep affection and appreciation of Dora's skills, I quietly began to look for ways to use my Human Resources position to benefit other qualified minority job candidates. I often identified opportunities for them. One aspect of that mission was certain: I never put an unqualified person anywhere they could fail. Success was important for them and for me to retain my position.

Brush Up Your Shakespeare

When the family moved out of the suburbs into New York City, I transferred to Marymount Manhattan College with a major in Drama. There, I totally immersed myself in the Broadway and off-Broadway theatre.

I studied music and acting outside of school as well. One of the acting classes was run by Nick Colasanto, an aspiring actor/director in his early 30's. He eventually found success on TV playing "Coach" the bartender in the popular TV series "Cheers". In the meantime his close friend, Ben Gazzara was appearing on Broadway in "Cat on a Hot Tin Roof." Ben at 27, enormously talented and charismatic was driven to excel at his craft, chase women and occasionally teach the class.

In this small group, I was the only one not struggling to survive. Living with my parents, I had access to a car and offered a lot of home cooked meals. I became something of a mascot to Nick and another friend of his, Mark Miller, a charming handsome Texan. He too later found success on TV appearing as the lead in "Please Don't Eat the Daisies." Ben also occasionally joined us at my home.

Nick lived in a Brownstone apartment on 52nd Street. One late evening, a gathering of about 10 talented actors sat around the fireplace, drinking and sharing stories. In this group Ben was the most successful and the other professionals did work sporadically. At one point a discussion of Shakespeare came up and Ben took center stage.

He picked up the play and started reading all the parts in "Othello." He read the lines as written and then translated them into the vernacular. He described Othello as "this Black guy, an extraordinary warrior worrying about fitting into regular society with his blue-eyed blonde wife. He succeeded on the battlefield and felt uncomfortable away from it. He was envied by many, particularly Iago, who set out to destroy him and did."

Ben captivated this audience of his peers. That night opened my eyes to the story and the beauty of the text. When I left, I found a copy of the play and re-read it. Later I went on to read all the major plays of Shakespeare. The music of the words and the strength of the stories added to my education. A psychiatrist friend once reminded me that everything is either in Psychology or Shakespeare.

Driving Dad

My father was sophisticated, successful and somewhat enigmatic. An engineer-entrepreneur, his companies in Washington, NY, Paris and Rome thrived. In his mid-sixties, he decided that having a combination chauffeur-valet would be "cool." So he found Joe, but where or how is a mystery.

Joe was Korean with limited English and, as it turned out, limited driving skills.

I was young, single, unemployed and living at home. As I have pointed out, my life consisted of parties, theatre, shopping, dating and some music lessons. Nothing remotely demanding.

One day my brother Arthur stopped by the apartment and told me:

"You have to drive Dad to Yonkers."

My question: "What's up, is Joe sick?"

"No, He's just a terrible driver."

"Are you joking? Doesn't Dad know that?"

"You think Dad knows anything about driving? Have you ever seen him drive a car?"

Actually I had once. It had been good for a funny story. Several years before, his friend was the designer of our new Studebaker and Dad wanted to try it out. My brother Bob and I took him to the empty parking lot at the railroad station in Greenwich. On the weekend no cars were around. The only vehicle on the lot was a huge semi-truck parked at the farthest end. Now at the wheel, Dad proceeded to drive this little car right in the direction of that big truck. The test ended abruptly when Bob yelled; "STOP" at the top of his lungs. Dad braked and Bob took over. We all laughed and went home for glass of wine.

No wonder no one wanted him to drive!

But what was the problem with Joe? Well, he liked to drive up First Avenue in the far left lane, before making a sudden right turn across four lanes to get to our apartment on Sutton Place. He also made a habit of parking illegally. He usually spent Monday evenings in Night Court.

After a while I became the designated driver. Joe was in the car with me so that parking would not be a problem. At day's end, I'd leave him at the subway.

Everyone joined in ribbing my father about Joe. The garage staff would not let him touch the car until it was on the street.

"Dad, you've got to get rid of Joe. He's just a joke."

"No, I can't. He's got a wife and children and needs the job."

This situation continued for a few months. Dora, our indispensable housekeeper, finally brought us closure. One evening Joe came into her kitchen to prepare a Korean dinner for us. He left her to deal with the total chaos he created.

The next morning Dora found my father at breakfast. Furious, with hands on her hips, she addressed Dad:

"Mr. Panero, it's Joe or me."

Without a moment's hesitation:

"Well Dora, I guess he'll have to go. We can't live without you around here."

If we'd only known that Dora was the key.

Call Me Guy

My father, as I have mentioned, was quite worldly and sophisticated. We, his loving children called him "Daddy." When we were all in our twenties, he asked each one of us separately to call him, "Guy." Bob and Arthur worked for him and perhaps, my father disliked the "Daddy" nickname in a professional environment.

I did not work for him and no way could I call him "Guy." After thinking about it, without consulting anyone, I switched to "Pop." Well, so did my brothers.

When my father realized we had unanimously decided on "Pop," his reaction: "I should have kept my mouth shut."

Poor "Pop" - no one of us could ever call our darling father "Guy."

Dad at Doubleday

We started living in the heart of Manhattan in 1955. Life now suddenly became exciting and being out of the suburbs, a great relief. In New York there is always someone to see, something to do, and plenty of friends.

The volunteer work at New York hospital kept me busy and dating a lot of interesting doctors and interns. At nineteen, being from a successful family, I could be considered a decent "catch". I left Marymount College and pursued random courses of General Studies at Columbia University.

Every night I spent time at the theatre, or dating, dancing, and totally enjoying life. At home my parents constantly argued. My father had maintained a long-term relationship with the widow of his mentor. It had gone on for years. He swore it had ended but someone reported to my mother that they had been seen together. My mother confronted my father, and threw dramatic temper tantrums every time she heard any rumors.

She would sometimes fall on the floor, kick and scream and yell. "You'll be sorry when I'm in St. John's." (The cemetery where all dead family members reside.) I tried not to listen and felt embarrassed for her. To me it was no way to behave, no matter what the circumstances. For my part, it was hard to live with.

One night out on a date with my one of my friends, we walked into Doubleday bookstore on Fifth Avenue. I saw Dad with the notorious Mrs. X and immediately backed out of the entrance, before they saw me.

The next day without calling I showed up at my father's office. It was on the 21st floor of the Greybar building over Grand Central Station. The office was spacious with a broad and bright sunny view of the City. When I walked in he was surprised and asked what I wanted.

"I want you to know that I don't care what you do, but last night I saw you in Doubleday with Mrs. X."

"What I do is none of your business."

"No, it is my business. Anyone of Mother's friends could have seen you and told her about it. Listening to you and mother constantly fighting is horrible. I hate it. You could find more private places to meet Mrs. X."

Visibly annoyed: "All you kids care about is my money."

"That's just not true. I can understand why you seek other company. I only ask that you be discreet, for my benefit if nothing else."

I persisted and made my father understand that his relationship with Mrs. X wasn't my business, as long as it is could be maintained in a quiet way.

I often wonder where my extremely liberal attitude came from. At any rate, he acknowledged the problem and agreed to be more discreet in the future.

I Need a Psychiatrist

When I worked as a volunteer at Payne Whitney psychiatric hospital, my own interior conflicts became apparent to me. I decided that I needed to see a therapist. I had no sense of purpose or idea where my life was taking me. Since I earned no money, my parents would have to foot the bill.

I decided to approach them. Not surprisingly they objected. "What are you talking about? You're not crazy."

I mentioned dropping out of college, having no purpose, and being generally confused. Nothing seemed to get to them.

Mother's reaction was the best. "That's nuts! There's nothing you can't tell your mother."

My unspoken response was: "Wanna bet?"

As I look back on that afternoon, I realize that at least my father listened. He gave me several good arguments to convince me that I was not a neurotic mess. "You have an active life, many interests and friends. There's nothing wrong with you."

Somehow, they finally agreed to let me see a doctor. I particularly wanted to talk to a Psychologist because from my volunteer experience I knew that Psychiatric residents did not necessarily have to study psychology. They would work with individual cases and be tutored by a senior Psychiatrist. In fact, when I was a secretary to one of the senior doctors, I did the research for his classes.

My first foray into therapy caused me to wake up and look at my conflicted ideas. I began to see and realize that it is not what happens to you that shapes your actions. It is what you think about it, that prompts behavior.

I participated in a group sessions led by Albert Ellis. He was among the first to push Cognitive Therapy forward.

In those sessions I was the only non-Jew. Everyone assumed that I too was Jewish and no remarks were censured. That group to a person believed and said that it was impossible to trust a Christian. My husband had even suggested that to me early in our marriage. "You'll get mad at me one day and call me a dirty Jew." I reminded him that I never argued in that way with anyone. My main prejudices revolved around unkindness, injustice or just plain nastiness. Then and now I only seek kind and intelligent friends.

Participating in that group, I realized how influenced we all are by our parents' words and examples. What they say and what they do become embedded in our minds and hearts. We are indoctrinated literally into a religion that can mold our thoughts permanently.

This experience shaped my thinking and gave me the ability to re-think ideas and to change. Therapy became an option whenever needed.

The Dating Scene

Returning from my junior year in Italy with new found self- confidence, I dated many men. In those innocent days, no one thought much about my antics. Because I volunteered at New York Hospital, I went out with a few doctors. Their hours were usually daytime and their workloads substantial.

I was unofficially engaged to one of the doctors until I met the man I married. I probably would have been happy to be his wife. We remained friends for many years. He was so smart, so funny and so confident.

On the party circuit another engaging personality was a restaurateur, Giorgio. We often started our evenings late, after I'd returned from a more normal evening. We would meet around 11 p.m. and maybe end the night around 3 a.m. Nothing closed early in New York City.

Giorgio's father owned an upscale restaurant on Wall Street. The family of one of his close friends owned the trendy and popular El Morocco. One could drink and dance through the night. Celebrities flocked there by the score. They could be seen or not. A private room in the back of the club protected anyone who wanted privacy. No reporters were allowed. Most of the prominent men there were with gorgeous women other than their wives.

Sometimes we would go out with the Maître D' from Giorgio's restaurant. His English was limited, and Giorgio wanted it to stay that way. We all spoke

Italian most of the time. Interestingly enough, when I visited Giorgio at his home in Florence, he spoke to me only in English.

His interest in me waxed and waned. While traveling with a friend in the summer of 1956 through Scandinavia and Germany, he called me from his home in Italy almost every day. His message "Come to Florence and spend some time with me."

I finally gave in and flew into Rome, caught a train to Florence and arrived in the middle of the night. Giorgio met me accompanied by two of his tiny, swarthy cousins. Both looked somewhat sinister, but they only came up to Giorgio's chin, so I didn't worry. Outside of the station, they ushered me into a long, black Cadillac limousine. We drove quietly through the city and into the hills. The light on the winding lanes up into the heights was limited. In the moonlight, the villa loomed large and ancient. It sat on the side of a hill overlooking Florence and Fiesole. It was late and Giorgio escorted me to my room. With a pristine peck on the cheek, he left me immediately. My room was beautiful with an enchanting view through the French doors that opened onto the balcony. The full moon shining low in the sky added to the evening's mystique. It is a vivid memory.

The next morning at breakfast, my host informed me that he would be away for a few days fishing with friends. If I wanted to, his Ford Thunderbird was mine to use for sight-seeing on my own.

After his avid pursuit, puzzled but not daunted, I set out. Fortunately, I had acquaintances in the area. With no experience driving in Europe, I gained some. Little did I know that driving less than 100 mph could be dangerous on the autostradas.

Looking back, I wonder at my nerve. Where did it come from? Maybe I was just brainless. Maybe no one said, "You can't do that." Maybe life is an adventure worth pursuing.

Living alone in this beautiful villa with his cousins waiting on me was strange, but the setting was lovely. I could read and call home to chat with my mother, who voiced her concern about my reputation.

"You're there alone with Giorgio? What will people think?"

"Well, he is off fishing with friends at the moment and even if he's here, there is an entire army of cousins chaperoning us."

My parents trusted me. I may have been spoiled in various ways but was not even remotely "wild". When Giorgio returned he took me to some interesting parties. He was smart and fun, and I enjoyed my short stay. When some old friends living in Rome asked me to visit them, I decided to leave before Giorgio headed off on another excursion.

After I left, he again started calling me every day, asking me to return. When I refused, he decided to come and see me in Rome. A very unusual man to say the least. My friends enjoyed his company and Giorgio stayed in Rome until I went home. He was confounding company but generous and entertaining. It appeared that if he wooed and won a person, he lost interest.

I did manage to realize that he was not a good bet for the long run.

Part II

Madly In Love

From their first reading of Cinderella, little girls long for their Prince Charming: I was no different. Although, many men pursued me, I never felt free to be myself. It was easier to be a chameleon. My values were so liberal, that I shared them with no one. It was 1960 and the Civil Rights movement was already important to me. My peer group was mainly white, anti-Semitic, and certainly not interested in rights of the Negro, as they were called in that era.

I met Frank, who would become my husband, at a party given by one of my South American friends: they wanted to introduce me to someone special. Instead, Frank came into my life.

When I met him, I was secretly engaged to a law student studying in Maryland. Frank had just returned from several years traveling as piano soloist with the United States Army Field Band. He was 5'9", handsome, with brown hair, big brown eyes and a golden complexion. Good looking as he was, I didn't particularly like him when we first met. He seemed vain.

This was a time when my numerous short engagements were beginning to annoy my parents. Those relationships seemed to last about three months. When Frank asked me out that same evening, I said yes, but first I took him home to meet my parents. I knew they wouldn't question me if I brought a guest to the apartment.

My brother Bob was with me when the three of us went to see my parents. Frank seeing the spinet in our living room tested it and then without an invitation sat down and played. It came alive and his music touched us all. We were awe-struck.

He and I stayed a while, until Frank offered to take me to dinner.

New York in June can be beautiful and this night, even though somewhat misty, lived up to its "Wonderful Town" reputation. We walked from Sutton Place in the East 50s down to the Battery. This part of town is now widely populated. It is at the tip of Manhattan. Then it was a quiet spot.

Chatting about everything, and nothing, the night took on a mystical charm. Since I had no real interest in dating Frank, I shared a lot of my liberal ideas with him. I didn't care what he thought about my beliefs and me because I was involved with someone else. I thought that by being myself, he would disappear.

When we reached the Battery, both leaning on the railing looking out into the glistening New York Harbor waters, Frank said, "There's no way you won't be part of my life." I was not interested at all. My inner thought was

"No way."

The next day he called and asked me out again. He sounded uncomfortable on the phone with me, and I gave him no help. Still I went out with him, mostly to hear him play again.

Frank asked me to concerts and I took him to various events and parties. He also often sat down and serenaded me with Chopin, Liszt, and Rachmaninoff. Music affects me more than any other art form. My reaction is visceral. Frank's moving interpretations particularly of Rachmaninoff captured my full attention.

A few weeks later, I remember sitting in a diner sharing a burger while Frank talked marriage to me. Finally, I said, "Listen, if you can keep me six months, you can have me."

"Do you have any idea how many women chase me?"

My answer: "How nice for you."

He had previously told me about a current romance with a violin player. I had watched other women flirt with him and even ask him out in front of me. I listened with no interest: jealousy is not my nature. You can't force love and you can't hold anyone's attention by being possessive. I've always been a great believer in everyone pursuing whatever dreams are important to him or her.

We continued to date even though we each saw other people. But, whenever I heard him play, it cast a spell. His good looks definitely added to his appeal. We passed the three-month mark and went forward. By Christmas, we wanted to be engaged formally. My parents offered no objections although Frank's parents had reservations because I was not Jewish.

My father, however, had other concerns. He presented them to me when we were alone one evening. He opened the conversation directly: "I don't want you to marry Frank unless you've slept with him. He is surrounded by homosexuals. You've been in Catholic schools where you've been taught that it's a sign of respect if a man doesn't touch you. It's not!"

I was in shock at my father's bluntness.

"You're wrong. They're not gay."

"Oh, yes they are."

My father was not homophobic at all. His male secretary was way out of any closet.

Finally, stunned, and speechless, I grabbed my throat and choked out. "It's OK. I did!" and dashed out of the room. He never brought it up again.

When I look back it's clear that I have no recollection of anyone objecting to Frank. At the time of my divorce, various friends commented on the fact that they had warned me not to marry him. Whatever anyone said to me is gone from my memory.

April in Paris

We became engaged at Christmas time, and a few weeks later my fiancé left for a concert tour in Europe. I was lonesome and sad to see him leave. My father felt sorry for me and loaned me his telephone card so I could call Frank in Europe. On the first call, we talked for about an hour as young couples in love do. I memorized the card number and proceeded to phone him on a regular basis- maybe as often as every other day. Those conversations were never short.

Frank concertized first in Sweden and then travelled to Spain and France. With my trusty memory of Dad's AT&T card, I trailed Frank telephonically across Europe.

About 6 weeks into Frank's tour, my father said he wanted to talk to me.

"Would you like to go to Europe? "

"Sure!!"

"You've spent quite a lot on phone calls. You could have been there and back more than once. It might be better if you went to Italy with your brother Bob and helped open the office in Rome. At least I'll save on telephone bills."

Dad didn't appear angry. Obviously, I was delighted to go to Italy to be closer to Frank.

Dad gave me a ticket to Rome with a layover in Paris. Little did he or my brother know that Frank was there. When the plane landed, we were to change aircraft for the last leg of the trip. Our party included Bob, his wife Vicki and their three small children. We disembarked and the family headed to the new gate. I disappeared through Customs. Bob, with a child on one arm and a baby seat under the other, saw me leaving and tried to stop me.

"Where are you going? Come back. "He couldn't leave his family and come after me without missing their plane. I did not spend time calculating his response.

I waved good-bye and disappeared.

There was my handsome fiancé waiting at the airport gate. He caught me up in his arms, with his warm, welcoming embrace. I loved the way he looked and felt. Hugging and holding hands, we went into town to immerse ourselves in the romance of April in Paris. What a joy!

We found a little hotel near the Arch de Triomphe, a bargain at about $6.00 a day.

We settled in quickly. We shared a tiny, narrow room with a view of the Champs Elyseé but you had to crane your neck a bit. The bed creaked and sagged. It was Heaven.

The upright piano in the small lobby gave Frank the chance to practice daily. Usually a small crowd would gather.

We watched the Algerian horse soldiers on parade...Men in the colorful robes of the desert riding astride a unit of black horses, followed by another unit on white horses. The robes in reds and whites, with flowing capes and turbans produced a dramatic scene fit for David Lean movie.

April in Paris: the weather added to our happy mood. During the day, we would walk the streets, living on bread, cheese and love. Almost every evening, we would be invited to dinner with friends. Frank had studied in Paris and his musical talent made us welcome in several homes. He never resented performing. As always, the music enchanted the audience and me.

Sometimes we found inexpensive restaurants and dined alone. All those days happily remain in my memory.

Being in love colors life in the rosiest hue. It was the most romantic time of my life – never be forgotten or regretted.

Honeymoon on Capri

Frank and I were living in Rome planning a July wedding. The fates intervened, or maybe I did. Frank's family was increasingly upset that we would marry in the Catholic Church. His parents had emigrated from Poland, experienced life in the ghetto and lost relatives in the holocaust.

Msgr. Cunningham of the Church of Santa Susanna in Rome had advised me to do all the paper work well in advance, in case problems arose. Early on, we satisfied the Italian civil requirements after spending a day at the Anagrafo (city hall). Then we dealt with the Church requirements. Oddly enough, there were not many problems from either of them.

Frank had decided we should marry in the Catholic Church, since it would bother me more than him. The problem arose when he started getting letters from his family. They let him know their extreme displeasure: in clear terms that no Christian can be trusted.

The pressure, even at a distance, affected Frank. He was ready to give up on our marriage and head back to the States. I came up with the idea to be married within a day.

"Your family will think it impossible to do that with all the Catholic rigmarole they've heard about."

I called Msgr. Cunningham to ask if we could be married that day. He said, "No, but I'll see you tomorrow morning at nine a.m."

We arranged it and then set out to tell my brother, since I worked for him.

Bob had invited us to a dinner party and nightclubbing that evening. I thought we could talk to him sooner, but it was one a.m. in the morning before we found a free moment. At last, he and his wife were sitting across from us in a nightclub.

"We're getting married tomorrow morning at nine o'clock and wanted you to know."

Dead silence.

"You're kidding." I tried to explain the problem, but Bob started making plans immediately.

"Pat, go back to your apartment and call Mother and Dad. I'm taking Frank with me. I'll pick you up in the morning."

They left and I headed back to my studio and started on a series of long distance calls. I'd talk... they'd shout and hang up...I'd call back ... more shouting, more hang ups. It went on for a few hours. I don't remember exactly what was said, but clearly no one was happy.

Bob came at eight a.m., and drove me to his nearby apartment. There, they put a veil on my head, handed me some flowers and off we went into the city. His chauffeur drove the two of us into Rome from suburban Parioli. During that half hour ride, Bob never stopped berating me.

"This is the stupidest thing you have ever done. I should have had you kidnapped and hidden in Sicily. This marriage will never work. He's the wrong person for you."

We finally arrived at the Church where almost 20 guests waited. My attendants were my sister-in-law, Vicki, my four-year-old niece, Helen and two other small children. We were married in the Sacristy with little ceremony. Everyone returned to Bob and Vicki's spacious apartment for a lovely lunch. Frank supplied the music of course.

At the end of the reception, Bob told me that Franco, his driver, would take us to Naples where we could catch a ferry and honeymoon on Capri. He had arranged everything. Talk about a "take charge" attitude. He obviously woke people in the middle of the night to have that many people appear.

We spent a lovely time on the wrong side of the Island in a small hotel overlooking the harbor. Frank practiced every day on their tiny out of tune piano. We would take the tram up to the main part of Capri and stroll through the streets where no cars were allowed. It was late June, but not crowded. We would sing to each other as we strolled up and down the narrow streets. Those days were magical.

Frank liked to hear me to sing Gershwin's "Summertime" and "Someone to Watch Over Me." Songs that are still my favorites. In a slightly off-key voice, Frank made me laugh with his rendition of "Ferdinand the Bull with the Delicate Ego."

One day the owner of the Pensione spoke to me about Frank's music. In Italian, she remarked how well he played for a movie star. I asked who she thought he was.

"Oh, I know he's John Saxon." I didn't deny it, since she was so happy to have a celebrity in her midst. (Saxon had been making a movie in Italy and they did somewhat resemble each other.)

A Trip through South and Central America- 1960

We were only married a few months, when the USIA contacted Frank and engaged him for a concert tour through South and Central America. Beginning in September it took him and me to Peru, Venezuela, Costa Rica, Nicaragua, Colombia, Cuba, Bolivia, and Honduras. Frank flew first class and my father treated me to an economy ticket.

Before the tour, after our honeymoon on Capri we went to Salzburg, Austria, where Frank studied at the Mozarteum. While there we were notified of two things: one that I was pregnant and the other, of the tour.

At our first stop in Lima, Peru, we met the embassy staff in charge of our trip. They sent us out alone with an itinerary that took us up the mountains to small towns, local concert halls, and questionable hotels at each stop. The poverty in view was striking as was the concert attendance. Every performance was standing room only, even in the poorest communities.

Frank spoke fluent Spanish and I managed to communicate with Spanish mixed with Italian. In one instance the mayor and the local B'hai missionaries sponsored us. After each performance the attendees and the locals entertained us. That particular mayor invited us to his unpretentious home to proudly show us that he had a real floor. Most homes and living quarters were rustic huts with dirt floors and outside plumbing facilities. The natives came to hear classical music, even those that lived with few of what we Americans considered necessities.

On the train from Lima that zigzagged up the mountains to altitudes of 12,000 or 14,000 feet, I watched an older looking man in a khaki uniform pace the corridors. With his safari hat sitting on top of his large head of white hair and a full mustachioed face, he carried under his arm an over-sized burlap bag that matched his clothes. I wondered what his job could be. I found out. As we climbed higher and higher, I began to feel my skin crawl. My breathing became shallow. Without asking, or any hesitation, this man appeared in front of me, put the bag's nozzle in my mouth and proceeded to hand pump oxygen into me. That was his job.

Returning to Lima, which is at sea level, presented a more normal setting. There I met a Jesuit missionary. After what I had seen in the hills, my youthful rashness took over and I asked him: "How can you justify proselytizing for Christianity with this type of poverty around you?" This impressive and imposing young man, cured my innate audacity permanently. He answered: "Listen, I'm just trying to get them to stop throwing virgins off the cliffs. OK!" I had no answer to that.

From Peru we went to Bolivia. We started out at small towns where the contrast between the rich and the poor was ever present. Again, the concert audiences filled every seat. In the small town of Oruro, a young girl came up to my husband at the end of his performance and asked "Are you Jewish?" When he said yes, she invited us to dinner at the Hotel Oruro which belonged to her father. This hotel was more of a rooming house with just six rooms and a small dining room. The daughter sat with us as we ate. Her father, Mr. Speigel, did not join us and barely spoke to us. Esther explained that he just wanted to entertain a Landsman with ties to the Jewish experience in the Europe he had fled. He had read that Frank's parents had emigrated from a Polish ghetto in the era of the Pogroms.

From there, we went to the town of Cochabamba, where Frank played at the Patino Palace. This magnificent building, home and concert hall, was designed by a French architect for Simon Patino, a millionaire who made his fortune in the tin market. The gardens surrounding the elegant house took their theme from the

Palace of Versailles. The reception following the concert featured the local gentry and many young women eager to flirt with my husband. One or two simply pushed me aside to find a chance to talk to him. My sense of humor bubbled up and I left them to chat with the German Ambassador, a 30 -year resident in Bolivia. His English was perfect and in our conversation, he told me that as a longtime resident in Cochabamba, he never left during World War II.

At the least, the striking privation existed in a town where flowers bloomed everywhere. This was, and probably still is, a beautiful city with buildings made of light colored stone that create the bright sunny look of Cochabamba.

From that town, we crossed the Altiplano to keep an appointment with the United States Ambassador in La Paz. The elevation on the dusty and dry Altiplano is about 13,000 ft. above sea level. We drove across that long dirt road in an old panel truck with the springs bulging out of the leather seats. On the way, the car began to break down. Our driver knew what to do. He asked Frank to drive while he sat on the bumper and poured some type of fluid into the carburetor. Who knows what it was! We almost made it to our destination before the car failed to operate. Our guide managed to leave us at the airport to find a cab to our hotel.

Sand and dust covered our clothes, hair and even our eyelashes. No rest stops existed on the road. When we at last arrived at our hotel, we quickly showered and headed for the Embassy. It looked like a movie set. The Ambassador, Mr. Carl Storm sat behind a majestic desk with flags furled behind him. An awesome figure, Mr. Storm greeted us warmly and thanked Frank for his musical success and our ability to easily connect with so many local people.

The two concerts in La Paz sold out. Several people stayed overnight in the concert hall. The music drew in the public and again, each concert was fully attended.

At our next stop in Caracas, an Embassy Attache remarked to me. "It's lucky you're not pregnant, American women naturally abort at those high altitudes." I said nothing and thought to myself, "How lucky I've always been."

As we visited each country, we witnessed the vivid contrast between great wealth and utter poverty. At each stop, we were entertained lavishly and other times with charming simplicity. Even with all the places I've been in this world, this short tour is to this day an experience without equal.

My brothers anticipating my birth

Baton Rouge, LA early 1940's

Coming out, NYC Gotham Debutante 1952

Family friends with me, London 1952

American co-ed Expeditionary Force bound for Europe 1952

The Italian Alps with me, 1954

The Panero Used Car Lot 1957

Paris 1960's: Bob

Paris 1960

Rome 1960

My brother Arthur, graduation photo

Guy with Aunt Vicky's cat, 1970

A cat I rescued, named Kat 1997

First Year of Marriage

My husband had married me believing I was rich. My father died within a year of our marriage and my son, Guy, was born. Three months after his birth I went to work as a secretary at a brokerage firm to bring in rent money. Just showing up and punching a clock was a challenge. This was 1961.

One broker I had known growing up in Greenwich, wouldn't acknowledge that he even knew me. The fact that I was working and had married a Jew made me unacceptable to some. Interestingly enough, it puzzled but didn't upset me. I was too happy with life. With no money, gorgeous music in the house, wonderful friends and an adorable, good-natured baby, I was more than content. It was the happiest time of my life.

After working for a year, the company cut salaries across the board. We lived on a strict budget, and losing the extra dollars, made me decide to look for another job. I found one in the hotel industry. It eventually led to a fascinating career in Human Resources.

Heading Home

I woke out of sound sleep, dreaming of the home I hadn't seen in a year. I heard my father's voice calling, "Come home, Pat." So clear. I rose letting Frank sleep on. Six months of constant travel, pregnant from day one of our marriage and just beginning to show, I suddenly just wanted to be home. Even though we would be back in New York within a week, I needed to leave Jamaica that day. When I picked up the local paper it headlined snow in New York City. That was it. Frank wouldn't mind, besides we'd be together in a week.

I dressed quickly, ran down to the concierge desk and arranged my ticket. Dad had paid my way for the past year, and wouldn't mind an extra charge.

Frank gave me no problem. I arrived in New York City within a few hours. My mother was waiting in Customs. She managed to charm the police officers and the customs agents into allowing her into the restricted Arrivals area. Those were the days...policemen were helpful and friendly. As the daughter of an Irish cop, she knew how to talk to them.

"My daughter is pregnant. I need to help her. She's been traveling for a year. I'm not sure she is even well. I want to be there when she leaves the plane." She found me at the baggage carousel. With immense joy, we threw ourselves at each other. Home at last!

With my father and mother, I enjoyed a marvelous week. We ate well, shared a few bottles of wine, and several stories of my adventures on tour. (In those days, no one told pregnant women not to drink.) It was a unique time, the three of us simply "catching up" and delighting in each other's company.

A Christmas Etched In Memory

Asleep and dreaming, I still hear my father's voice calling me. "Come home."

Now here I stood, looking out into the midnight sky and the city of New York. New York Hospital sits in a prime location overlooking the East River. The waiting room has a beautiful view. The sight of the shimmering river and the city with its lights ablaze, captured my heart even in the midst of grief. How many people have stood here through the years? How much sadness has lived in this place?

My father is down the hall in a coma. Even if he survives, he will not live long. Of that I am sure. It's Christmas time and at least both my brothers are in town.

I'm glad that I left Frank to finish his tour and had come home early to see my parents and the promise of a white Christmas. As a family, we had an instinct for good stories, good food and good fun. My parents and I had enjoyed the week together. My father's health had been deteriorating over the last year and at the end of this week, it fell apart completely.

On the day Frank returned from Jamaica, Dad was rushed to New York Hospital with cardiac arrest. From that day on, he was in and out of distress and never the same. To watch him die by inches tortured all of us. He had ruled the family, quietly, but firmly. Without him, everything changed.

He suffered from a disease called hemochromatosis. It had gone undiagnosed for several years. It causes excess iron to be deposited in different organs of the body. It results in Diabetes, and cirrhosis of the liver. In time, I learned that it is inherited but only affects men. The cure is simple enough if diagnosed. It requires old-fashioned bleeding.

Growing Up

What is it like to grow up rich with every privilege and then lose it all? Not as bad as one might think.

My father made a great deal of money and had warned me that when he died it would be gone. At his death, his Will left my two older brothers in charge. There were four companies to manage and with that income they were to take care of my mother and me. My father had no idea how much they disliked each other. They fought constantly. They were able to sell the United States companies before destroying them. The offices in Rome and Paris did not survive.

The large amount of life insurance left only to my mother, she loaned to my brothers to protect the company. As a result - I ended up working and supporting my mother and my own little family.

I had never really worked except for my father and that was more like having long lunches with him and his former colleagues.

Because my parents never wanted me to take a job away from someone who needed it, I had never felt a sense of purpose. In that era, it was generally accepted as the way women were educated. I learned to speak passable French and decent Italian. I developed a deep and permanent love of the Arts. Nothing was really expected of me. Oddly enough I was taught tolerance and respect of all people, regardless of their status in life. My parents valued talent, intelligence and character. Also, they never suggested that I was entitled to my privileges.

My first experience with higher education was at Manhattanville College. I dropped out just before the end of the first semester. I wanted to be on the stage and enrolled in the Feagin School of Drama located at Rockefeller Center. The experience opened my eyes to the outside world. The school was led by Mrs. Feagin and her daughter and son-in-law. The students were from various parts of the country and to even my inexperienced eyes, appeared untalented, uneducated and unintelligent. That six months drove me right back to school.

The next year I re-entered as a freshman at Newton College of the Sacred Heart and began to understand that I had potential. The school was in Massachusetts and away from the family influences. For the first time I stood out as a something of a leader. However, it was clear I only took charge when no one else wanted to.

A problem arose when my father became ill. My parents moved from Connecticut to New York City and I transferred to Marymount Manhattan College. Living in New York City back in the family fold did nothing to foster my independence.

Life in the City was wonderful; yet having everything can be boring. I studied singing, acting, read constantly, lunched, went to the theatre, shopped, volunteered, dated, and went to school when I felt like it. There was definitely no direction to my life. I wanted to sing professionally but that was not acceptable to my parents. Their message: appreciate what I have and help others in need. Volunteering became a way of life and still is.

A Most Important Job

I started working in 1961. With limited experience my only option existed at the entry level.

My typing fell short of excellent, fast scribbling replaced steno, but my phone skills surpassed most applicants. I spoke rudimentary Spanish and fair Italian. It looked good enough on paper. My father's company served as a "Last Employer", now that my name changed. My uncle who worked there, agreed to be my reference and exaggerate a bit about my ability.

A small personnel office in a Wall Street firm hired me as a secretary. The company was fading and the work load was non-demanding. There was not much to do. After a year when they cut my salary by $5.00 a week, I decided to look for something else. We needed the $5.00.

Interviewing for a job as secretary to the Corporate Director of Personnel for Loews Hotels, Douglas Pierce brought up the issue of my small child. I explained that my husband stayed home until the afternoon, my mother lived nearby, and it was not a problem. He kept shaking his head in a "no way" mode. When I mentioned my Spanish skills, he gave in.

It was unusual for someone with my background to be looking for a job. When I look back, the cultural change is startling. He hired me with the caveat, "The minute you call in sick because your child has a problem, don't bother to come back."

The only time my son Guy was ill, I caught a cab at lunchtime and returned in an hour. It helped to live in the City and be near work. It also helped that Guy was healthy with an easy–going temperament and always slept through the night.

Mr. Pierce decided to give me a chance as he liked the idea that living in New York City, I could open the office every day.

In the meantime, every morning at least 100 people stood outside the door waiting to apply for jobs. The company had rented a huge space in the West Fifties near the hotel being built. Our four desks sat at the back of the enormous space. Banquet tables were set up near the front where people filled out applications.

I opened the door each day and let the crowd in. Since I was there first, I began talking to people and asking them to explain their jobs and their job titles.

"Describe a day at work as a dishwasher. Tell me what does a bottle breaker do exactly?" This union hotel had dozens of job categories all a mystery to me: garde manger, sous chef, poissonier, bottle breaker just to name a few. I began thoroughly interviewing everyone who had position titles unknown to me.

It is clear that when someone likes their job, they can talk about it endlessly. Our candidates educated me and I referred the best of them to the department heads. I learned more and more. Each day flew by and my reputation for finding qualified and motivated staff grew.

An interesting issue faced me one day. I was charged with finding telephone operators and my first applicant asked: "How many positions does your board have?" Startled, I began to visualize... sitting down, standing?? I gave up.

To find the answer I approached our chief operator. She, a crusty, smart, very Irish supervisor from Queens had no fondness for me. Her curt answer to the question: "twelve." Now totally confused but afraid to ask for an explanation, I went back and told the candidate 12." Her reply: "Well, I've only done 10, but I can handle it."

At this point I concluded the interview. I did not know what to think; so many women in so many positions.

Incidents like this increased my insecurity daily, but I kept working on my interviewing skills.

After the first two weeks, Mr. Pierce called me into his office.

"How do you think you're doing so far?"

My honest answer got his attention.

"I have no idea what I'm doing."

"You're right. You don't. You act as if you do."

"Please don't fire me. I'll get better quickly and I really need the job."

"Okay, let's see what next week is like."

Then he took me over to my desk, opened the bottom drawer and went on to the next subject.

"What are all these unanswered letters in here?"

I told him that all my time was spent interviewing, and he did understand.

He chose to hire a temporary secretary for me. She made $25.00 a week more than I. She was an attractive, smart young English girl with top notch skills. Penelope took great care of my boss and me. Even though she reported to me, I never told her how to do her work. I listened carefully to everything she said, and followed her lead. Another lesson learned: when someone can do something better than you can, let them. Remember to give them public praise and if called for, see that they are promoted.

I loved my job and relished the challenge of constantly learning. My hours were from 8:30 a.m. until 7 pm and the days flew by. In the meantime, I changed my small child's sleeping pattern to spend more time with him. He now rose at noon and went to bed at midnight. This job was the beginning of a life-time career in the hotel industry.

After a while, my boss realized my interviewing skills were more valuable than my secretarial prowess. After a few months, he informed me that my ability to select good candidates was the best he had ever seen.

From that job, I not only acquired interviewing skills, but the ability to solve problems. After a while I understood and could staff almost any position in a hotel.

To succeed in the hotel industry enormous energy and a desire to serve are essential. My first job with Loews Hotels gave me my love for the industry.

Is It Xmas Or Christmas?

Esther, my fiery Jewish mother-in-law used to get annoyed with the phrase "Happy Holidays." Her line "For God's sake, it isn't going to kill me to hear Merry Christmas."

Esther, barely 5 feet tall, with bright red (almost orange) hair, fair skin and big dark eyes, was quite pretty and extremely smart. Though she was leery about her Christian daughter-in-law, we definitely respected each other. We remained close even after I left her "do no wrong" son.

She and her husband Abe had come from Poland to escape the Pogroms. With limited schooling, and unlimited aspirations, they opened a Sweet Shop in Fairlawn, New Jersey. The shop sold comic books, candy and food served at a counter. Abe did most of the cooking and Esther took care of the customers. From that small store, they managed to give their talented son a first class international musical education. Frank studied in Paris, Austria, Spain and the United States.

While Frank and I were married, we all enjoyed the mixed up celebrations of Christmas and Chanukah. My heritage included the mandate to entertain and include people for any and all celebrations. Esther's heritage was love and loyalty to family and its traditions.

At one gathering in her home, my 18-month-old son asked his Grandma:

"How come Uncle Morris never talks to Mommy?"

She stopped, thought about it a moment, and answered: "He will!"

Esther cornered her brother immediately after Guy's comment. She let him know that he was unwelcome in her home unless he managed to greet and maybe even speak to me. She, the family matriarch changed his attitude. He decided to talk to me, although not much.

It took a little time, but she and I became friends. An enthusiastic, proud and loving grandmother, she took her three grandchildren from their earliest years, to the ballet, theatre and symphony.

Her grandchildren adored her and she returned the affection. She imparted her love of music and the arts to all three of them. In my case, she was the first person who identified potential in me. She amazed me one day when she said, "If you'd been my daughter you would have a singing career."

Through her eyes, I understood the immigrant's strength of character. She worked hard for the benefit of her children and her siblings. Her integrity and character were ever present. She showed me how important it is to work to achieve goals - something no one had ever pointed out to me.

How could you not love her? I miss her.

I am now the "older" generation hoping my grandson will feel the same way about me someday.

Salesmen

A lot can happen in a year. After we returned to NYC in December, our son was born in March and my father died in May.

Suddenly we had little money and no home. We took over the apartment of Frank's music professor which meant sharing it with two other students. A large six room apartment on the West Side of Manhattan housed all of us. It was not then as chic and trendy as it today.

The living and dining room opened up to 60 feet of space, and was perfect for informal musical gatherings. Two grand pianos fit easily at one end. If you closed the door between the two large bedrooms, you could not hear when either or both pianos were being played.

Frank and I moved into one of the bedrooms with our tiny baby. The two male students stayed with us, while they looked for new lodgings. Not one of us made housekeeping a priority.

Because the apartment needed to be cleaned, I contacted Electrolux and asked to have a salesman demonstrate their products.

The salesman arrived one afternoon. I was still dressed in maternity clothes and the baby lay asleep in his bassinet, in the dining room. The young man introduced himself and then was concerned he'd make too much noise.

"Don't worry. With a grand piano being played at all hours, this baby will have to get used to noise."

"Okay then. Let me show you how efficient this machine is."

I let him vacuum the living room without giving any sign of approval. I wanted him to finish cleaning the dining room before a decision was made.

"I'll have to talk to my husband about this."

In the meantime, one of the boarders came through the door, greeted us and disappeared.

"Is that your husband?"

"No."

Then about 10 minutes later, the other young man came home. He said "Hi" and went to his room.

"Is that your husband?"

"No."

"When is he here?" At this point the salesman looked uncomfortable and had done a fair amount of vacuuming.

I had to think a bit.

"Um, usually on Tuesday afternoon."

The guy looked at me in amazement, emptied the dirt from the vacuum on the floor, packed up quickly, gave me his card and left. He said:

"Call me when you want to buy it."

It didn't dawn on me until later what a strange scene I had presented. Thinking about how it appeared to him, I can only laugh. Anyway, I did call and did buy the Electrolux. That particular salesman, however, never did come back.

End of a Marriage

Frank, the man I married, was the best friend I ever had. His good-looks and his musical talent made him irresistible to me. The first years' time spent traveling through Europe and touring South and Central America were easy. We were totally compatible and never fought.

Having a child changed our relationship: first, in subtle ways and later on profoundly. It also changed me. For example: I was going to save money and use a clinic for pediatric care. Then an intern came to me the second day of my son's life. He said: "The baby has an infection of unknown origin and a fever. "At that moment, I called Dr. Henry Goldberg, the best pediatrician at New York Hospital. We knew each other as he had cared for my nieces and nephews. He came to the hospital the next day and let me know there was nothing wrong with baby Guy. The infection and fever were not uncommon to newborns. A first rate doctor is worth any cost.

I learned immediately that infants require one's total attention. I also learned that my husband resented that fact. I had never seen Frank's ego clearly.

Also as the years passed, I found elements in his character that caused me to lose respect for his judgment in certain areas. I worked, gave him my paycheck and he managed our lives. His frugality bothered me but I said little about it. He studied piano and taught, but my salary was the major contribution.

Over time I felt increasingly trapped. I quit my job with one company because I wanted less prominence. I thought my marriage would be better served if I was not obviously successful. The new job I found was boring, paid more but offered almost no challenge.

My home life was enriched by love of music, delight with my son, strong friendships and a fondness for entertaining. It was one way to see that the house was clean and organized regularly. Always an indifferent housekeeper, early in my marriage, I wondered why the waste paper baskets were so full. Frank said: "You have to empty them." I honestly did not know that.

Even though I was a terrible cook my parties worked. I served strong drinks and ordered from the wonderful restaurants in our West Side neighborhood. Those parties solidified many friendships that still last. Among our friends were two couples to whom we were particularly close. We women had known each other before marriage. Their husbands were interesting, intelligent and fun. Frank's music was appreciated by all of us. When each of the couples left the city for new jobs, I realized how much intellectual stimulation they provided. Frank did not read as much as I, and outside of the music, we had little in common. I began to feel lonely. I decided to try seeing a counselor.

Group therapy is educational. I learned that it is not what happens to you but what you think about it. As I explored ideas with my therapist, I asked him to include Frank in our discussions. After meeting him once, my doctor told me that Frank was happy and did not see any problems.

The last year of my marriage several events led up to my decision to ask for a divorce. Once at a party of a close friend and art lover, Frank decided to buy a painting being offered. I told him: "If you buy that painting, it will be the end of our marriage." I knew I would have to pay for it.

A few weeks later, Frank barely consulting me, found a house in New Jersey and with his parents help, bought it. We moved and this meant three hours daily commuting to the city. One day leaving work, I suddenly grew numb on my right side. I needed help getting home, as my gait was unsteady. The next day, imagining the worst, I called my doctor. He saw me immediately. He examined me for fifteen minutes, took me to his office and said: "You do not have cancer or a brain tumor. You are suffering from extreme nervous tension. I can give you tranquilizers or you can solve your problem." I did not need to think about it. I thanked the doctor and let him know I'd solve the problem.

I walked out of the office and phoned my brother, Arthur.

"I want a divorce and need a lawyer as soon as possible."

Arthur asked no questions. He said he'd get back to me.

Arthur found me a lawyer quickly. This was May and I wanted to leave at the end of June. My lawyer asked why I wanted a divorce. I wanted to be free. I did not like the long commute. I did not want to help pay for a way of life that took me out of the City and away from friends. I wanted custody of my son, but was willing to see that he spent time with his father. The lawyer drew up an equitable Separation Agreement valid in New York State. With that in hand, a Mexican divorce was able to be scheduled.

Before I left in September for Mexico, I wanted my brother Bob to know. I arranged to meet him for lunch at his favorite New York City restaurant to tell him my plans. He came as usual with a small retinue of friends. Finally, when we were only three people, I couldn't wait any more. I interrupted the conversation:

"I'm getting a divorce."

His immediate reaction: "Congratulations!!"

Then he stood up, called the waiter and announced to everyone still in the room. "Champagne for everyone." I can still hear his voice.

No one made it back to the office that day.

The marriage lasted nine years. It was as if I had been in jail. I never looked back and never regretted leaving Frank.

Part III

Raising Guy

My bright, talkative son radiated energy and intelligence. Raising him without a father present sometimes challenged my patience. However, my sense of humor saved my sanity.

After divorcing, my mother, Guy and I moved into New York City. I chose the neighborhood of First Avenue and 79th Street because P.S. 158 was considered the 2nd best public school in the city. I couldn't afford a private school. Guy was considered "IGC" (intellectually gifted) and put in a special class. It happened that many of those students were boys. On weekends, I took three or four of them to various events. I didn't want an isolated "only child."

In New York City, Central Park offered bicycling, skating, ball games, horseback riding and benches to sit on. Sometimes, we went ice-skating at Rockefeller Center. The city has movies, museums and McDonalds. The boys were easy to deal with. My line to them: "I expect you all to behave like princes or you'll never come with us again." It worked perfectly.

Occasionally helping Guy with homework, I noticed the teacher making corrections that were incorrect. It began to bother me. I scheduled a student conference with her, but when I appeared, she burst into tears.

"Mrs. Sherr, I know you take the boys everywhere. How do you deal with them?"

She cried on my shoulder. Bright young children are definitely creative in dreaming up mischief. Her young charges were much brighter than she. It is at that point I decided private school might be a better option.

One day, Guy and a friend came to our 2nd floor apartment with ropes and pulleys. They went into Guy's small bedroom overlooking 79th Street. I called Guy aside immediately.

"You and your friend are not going to lower yourselves out the window!"

"How did you know we were gonna to do that?"

Obviously, an easy guess, but it left the boys wondering if I was clairvoyant.

This small band of boys came up with all sorts of ideas. One involved running up the wall from the bed and seeing how far they could get on the ceiling before falling back. The footprints on the ceiling told the story and kept score.

Another time, when our doorman gave me four tickets to a ball game at Yankee Stadium, I took Guy and his two friends, Eric and John with us. We were split up on different sides of the stadium. I told Eric and Guy exactly where and when to meet John and me at game's end. When we got there, they were missing. It began raining as I found a young policeman and told him my problem.

"Oh ma'am, I'm sure they wanted to try and make it home on the subway by themselves."

Now I'm really upset. These two boys looked like East Side rich kids, traveling through Harlem alone. The policeman suggested I contact Eric's mother to see if they were home. That was not a good idea. She and I were barely acquainted and she seemed the nervous type.

John and I grabbed a cab and headed back to 79th Street. Yes, the cop was correct. They wanted to try the subway alone.

The boys said:

"Well, you weren't there and we thought we'd just go home."

I said: "Any time I'm not where I tell you to meet me, I'm either dead or unconscious, call the police."

When I made the decision to put Guy in a private school, St. David's was my choice. Being in Human Resources taught me how important a good education is.

I had no idea if Guy could succeed in a more rigorous system and when talking to the headmaster, I told him I'd have Guy tutored if necessary.

In the meantime, I did not try to prepare Guy for his interview at school. I did however point out that Willie Mays' son went there, a big plus to my baseball fanatic son.

We show up for the interview, and I was shocked at Guy's response to a certain question.

"What are your favorite TV programs?"

"Oh, my mother doesn't let me watch TV. "(Not even close to the truth.)

He answered every question as if I had prepared him: I still wonder how he knew these responses were the key.

At the end of this aced interview, Mr. Dryzga asked Guy if he had any questions.

Guy said: "Does Willie Mays' son go to school here?" (Looks like he was checking my veracity.)

The answer was yes and St. David's accepted Guy with no tutoring needed. It was a wonderful school and Guy loved it.

Lost In Central Park

A child brought up in New York City develops street smarts without much prompting.

Living in Manhattan with a young boy it was impossible to manage him every second. All I could do was to enroll him in sports and instruct him in safety measures.

Children need to know their phone number and their address. Nowadays they have cell phones, but they didn't exist then. Once when Guy was separated from his father in Central Park, he found a person to take him to the bike shop where he had started out. He called me and I came and picked him up. In the meantime, Frank called me too. When I asked Guy how he selected the person to help him, his answer was "He dressed like you and Daddy do."

Another time, he and I lost each other biking in Central Park. Now he was older. I immediately found the nearest mounted policeman to report him missing.

"My 10 year-old is missing. He is not too tall with a mop of bright red hair. His name is Guy."

"I'll radio it in, Ma'am."

After a short wait, the policeman let me know that Guy was at the Boat House in the company of another officer. I walked there and found Guy in lively conversation with his protector.

As I approached, Guy ran over to me. "I told the policeman you would put out an APB on me. We just had to wait."

The officer came over and congratulated me on educating my son for emergencies. Now I started laughing. Guy had figured it out without my help. He knew I'd find a policeman and knew enough to stay in one place.

City kids learn on their own about maneuvering in cities.

They know the bus drivers, shop keepers and doormen on whatever routes traveled. Occasionally riding with my garrulous son on the crosstown bus, Guy would even introduce me to the driver.

"Mom, this is Joe, we had him twice yesterday. Joe, this is my mother."

Once when a school chum visited us, he told me how scared he was of the mini muggers who came out of Harlem. They preyed on the private school kids, easily identified by their grey pants and blue blazers. When I asked Guy why he never mentioned this, he answered,

"It doesn't bother me."

"Why not?"

"I'm not rich."

"They may not know that, so be careful."

Questioning him further, I found out that waiting for buses on Madison Avenue, Guy would go into some of the shops and engage the staff in conversation. He knew all about the recession and picked up and shared a few sales tips with me.

In those days, New York City blocks provided as much of a neighborhood as a small town. A bowling alley was a block away from us. Guy was known to the owners. They let him play, knowing that I would take care of the cost. Living in New York City, it is smart to know your neighbors and the neighborhood.

I also let Guy play at the local pool hall. He loved the game, was good at it and very little could disrupt his concentration. There again, owners knew him and me as neighbors. City kids also knew they had to keep their parents informed of their whereabouts and usually traveled with at least one companion.

Walking on the streets with Guy one day, he was far ahead of me playing with his yo-yo. A boy, a head taller, not from the area came up beside him and made threatening remarks. Guy said nothing but kept the yo-yo in play, never missing a beat. I moved closer but the young boy disappeared.

"Not to worry, Mom...I knew he'd leave if I did nothing." How he knew this surprised me. Growing up in a city can have many advantages, especially if parents know their children and their neighborhoods.

Skating At Rockefeller Center

From my early years, skating at Rockefeller Center was a family tradition. My parents often brought me there for lessons. Mr. Peters was the skating instructor. Originally from Norway, handsome, he was tall and fit with enormous patience.

One day I decided to take Guy and his friend Eric ice-skating at Rockefeller Center. The boys were ten years old. Eric was my favorite. He had a head full of unruly ash blonde curls, a slight build with big eyes magnified by his glasses. He had the sweetest disposition. I just loved him.

We headed for the rink one afternoon, rented our skates and hit the ice.

Eric was in fact the only one who didn't hit the ice. As he entered the rink, he began losing his balance, but arms waving and flailing about he stayed upright. However, he couldn't stop and began plowing into people. He reminded me of a fair-haired Charlie Chaplin. I went to help him and he brought me down too, but still never hit the ice. My old friend Mr. Peters came to the rescue and he too went down. I grabbed the railing and watched Eric skating around the oval and upsetting anyone near him. I could not stop laughing. There was no way to remain "cool." Guy after a few falls came up beside me. "What can we do? "

Mr. Peters joined us. "No one has ever made me fall before". He too chuckled. We made a plan and finally the three of us ended Eric's personal ice capade. We went home and all was well. The memory will never, never leave me.

The Knickerbocker Greys

In New York City, the "Greys" served as a marching troop for young boys. This elite group provided after school activities for the sons of many famous people. I became acquainted with them the day my 10-year-old son came to me.

"Mom, The Greys want me to join them."

"Who are they, a family at school?"

"No, a military unit for kids. Mrs. Murray said she would call you."

At this point, I remembered this group included Truman's grandsons, Rockefeller kin and a long list of social register types. The boys' connections went back to organizations celebrating the Colonial, Revolutionary and/or Civil Wars. The Grey's attracted the elite of New York City. Never have I been enamored of ancestor worship, even as a debutante. People feeling entitled because of ancestry did not interest me.

Mrs. Murray, a Park Avenue denizen, did indeed call.

"Mrs. Sherr, the Greys would like to have Guy join them in their activities." This invitation was delivered with the charming, distinctly upper class accents of the East Coast.

"Thank you so much for the invitation, but the cost would be prohibitive for me right now."

"Oh, don't worry, we will give him a scholarship and you can just provide for the uniforms."

Not really approving of the organization, I declined still citing the expense.

"Oh, well, then we'll see that he has uniforms. Could you possibly meet me for a short interview at the Park Avenue Armory one day? We can complete the admission process."

Now, there was no way to decline. Guy wanted to be part of the group and the money issue no longer existed.

The Armory is on Park Avenue and 67th Street. The steps leading up to the entrance are perhaps 20 in number. Guy and I arrived for the meeting promptly at 2 p.m. The tall, beautiful and elegant Mrs. Murray waited at the top. She had the hairstyle of the day, shoulder length with a flip at the end, the type hairspray guaranteed would stay in place.

When Guy saw her, he raced up the stairs, shouting: "Mrs. Murray, Mrs. Murray." She stretched out her arms and hugged him enthusiastically. As I arrived at the top of the stairs she shook my hand, welcomed me and spent the rest of her time concentrating on Guy. She was polite but needed only a short conversation with me. My guess, she probably wanted to make sure I was not a troll.

The Greys inducted him into their troop and he loved it. I also loved watching the kids march on the Armory floor. Guy even brokered another scholarship for a friend of his.

Guy's charm and ebullience amazed others and delighted me.

Mother's Death

Christmas time in 1971, I was fired from my job as an Executive Recruiter because of policy disputes. At the same time, it became clear that my mother's health was failing. She had colon cancer. I found a low paying, non-demanding job immediately. It was important to be more available at home with my lively 11 year-old and his sick grandmother. This was a complicated existence for all of us.

Guy was enrolled in St. David's school and the thought of paying next year's tuition worried me. I also did routine jobs, typing, temporary receptionist, filing insurance claims, to add to my income.

Even though those days were depressing, my love for and ability to take care of Guy and mother, kept me going.

In the spring, mother wanted to spend a week visiting friends in Florida. It became a turning point for her. When she returned, she said:

"So many of my rich widowed friends are leading lives of comfort and ease and are all alone. Many are alienated from their children and preoccupied with money and clothes. Here I am having a very happy old age with you and Guy and that's what life is all about. I never want to leave home again."

When she returned much weakened, Guy welcomed her with hugs, kisses and attention. I eavesdropped on their conversations and found them moving.

"Grandma you are so beautiful." He sat and talked to her and they consoled each other about how strict I was. She told old and new stories of her life. His sensitivity and kindness to her was awesome. This difficult time was made easier for me watching the two of them.

Regardless of all the problems, we were lucky to have each other.

I sent Guy away to camp in the summer and put my mother in the care of the Dominican nuns' hospice care. She died peacefully in October. I did not want Guy to watch her die bit by bit. This was a mistake. He was angry at me.

"You never cried, you didn't love Grandma."

I apologized: "I didn't want to upset you. I thought if I cried in front of you, it would be worse. I'm sorry. I made a mistake. From now on I'll cry in front of you."

After I arranged the funeral and the viewing, I took Guy by himself to see her in the open casket. I watched as he touched her, and spoke to her. No one else was with us. He decided when we would leave.

Many years later when I mentioned how profoundly her death affected him: he said: "Don't be silly I haven't thought about her for days."

Grace under Pressure

I lost my job during an economic downturn in 1970. My divorce lawyer referred me to a friend, the Chief Operating Officer of a cosmetic company affiliated with Revlon. To qualify for the job, I first stopped in Personnel for an interview with a typing and steno test. For the test, I was asked to take dictation and then transcribe it. I scribbled fast but missed part of the letter. They sent me into a small cubicle to type up my results. There I found all the answers in a full waste paper basket. Typing slowly and correctly, I passed and was hired as secretary to the Director of Finance.

In this odd environment women held the major leadership positions. They were smart, competitive and as executives, outside the realm of my experience. I needed the job and was grateful to have it even with a large pay cut. Because of my ability to analyze and solve problems, understand individual priorities and meet deadlines, I got promoted rapidly.

My title, Head of the Beauty Treatment Institute (a one-person department) sent me out to department stores to educate the public on what make up and skin care products to use. My closest friends were impressed and asked for advice. My response,

"I knew nothing yesterday before they gave me the title. Let me see what I can find out."

An appointment with the staff dermatologist enlightened me.

My question: "What can a person do to ensure an excellent complexion?"

Dr. Smith: "Choose your grandparents very carefully and stay out of the Sun."

He then briefed me on the products Revlon sold and how to use them. I did learn that proper packaging meant higher prices.

Next, to prepare me for my guest appearances, they sat me in a chair, plucked my heavy eyebrows to a thin line, added false eyelashes, and in general added my concept of a ton of makeup. My long dyed blonde hair was appropriately teased, to match the style of the day. This trendy look was time consuming to produce.

I went to Saks and Bonwit Teller and talked to a great many people. It was easy to advise on makeup if they had my coloring – fair complexion, blonde hair and blue eyes. I relied on the knowledgeable sales staff to teach me about other types of combinations. It startled me when dark-haired, dark-eyed women with olive skin tones, would say: "I want the same look that you have." To me they looked lovely.

I stayed with the company for a while. Eventually I was offered a job with a recruiting firm and accepted it. The salary was good and I was delighted to stop teasing my hair and wearing fake eyelashes.

There Is a Free Lunch

After my mother died, I started to search for a management job in Human Resources. My resume did not help much. The last two years were inconsistent and complicated to explain in an interview.

One particular day, depressed and low on cash, I called a general manager friend and asked him to treat me to lunch. Skip Hartman had been Corporate Director of Personnel at Loews Hotel Corporation when I reported to him. We always got along.

Now the General Manager at the Drake Hotel in New York City, we met and went into the dining room. As we sat down he said:

"Good thing you caught me. I'm leaving next week for Washington to open a new hotel, Loews L'enfant Plaza."

As I sat down, I said:

"Would you hire me as your Personnel Director?"

"Sure, but the job may not last too long. You'll have to negotiate your salary and relocation with the corporate office."

I immediately told him that he had made my day. I was glad to return to the hotel industry, glad to open another hotel, and glad to work for him. Moving to Washington was a real plus. Guy's father was there as were three very dear and close friends. Life would only be better for both Guy and me.

I managed to end my lease and make a short visit to Washington. With the help of my friends, Alan and Martha McDonald, I found an attached four-bedroom, three story townhouse in Bethesda, Maryland. It cost half of my New York apartment. Guy and I arrived in January 1973, the week before my job started. After paying the movers, I borrowed $100.00 from the McDonalds until my first paycheck.

Opening the hotel was time consuming, challenging and exciting. My boss's wife occasionally added my son to their household of two children. They were all roughly the same age. At times, I let Guy work on the plug board telephone system in the hotel. Our chief operator let me know that he was her best operator, when in an emergency situation, she made me go home and bring him in to work.

My nephew Arthur came to visit that summer. Guy was away with his father. Arthur asked if I could find him a job, and I put in the Room Service Department. We drove into the city each morning and he made his way back alone in the evening.

When he wanted a weekend job as well, that was easy as he had gained a reputation as a hard worker. I was able to place him in the garage as a valet parker.

When driving him in one weekend, he said:

"My friends say you're crazy to drive me to work every day of the week."

My response: "Do you want me to stop? "

"No."

"Then just say thank you."

This started a conversation where Arthur let me know he never met an adult he could trust until he met me and Martha McDonald who lived nearby. Arthur never asked to go back home to Florida, and I never wanted him to leave.

Another summer when Guy was away camping with his father, my nephew Patrick, the son of my other brother, came to visit for a few weeks.

Living with the two of them was entertaining. Patrick read books all day and wanted us to go out to eat at night. Arthur and I were too tired. In desperation, Patrick asked for a job. I hired him as a laundry attendant, an uninteresting job but he only had to do it for a month or so before returning to school.

One day in the hotel, I decided to go down to the basement to see how he was doing. I found him lazily sorting a huge stack of hotel linens while lying on top of them underneath the giant laundry chute. A dangerous place to be, - anything can come shooting down the 14 flights at any moment. Patrick got up when reminded of that.

The day Guy returned, I yelled at him about some minor problem. His response: "Don't waste your breath, I have no idea what SOP (Standard Operating Procedure) is around here anymore."

After Patrick returned to school, life with Guy and Arthur resumed its amusing quality. Guy, 5'6" weighed around 125 lbs., Arthur, 6ft tall, weighed a lot more. One day when Guy talked back to me in the kitchen, his cousin picked him up and pinned him to the wall.

"Don't talk to your Mother like that or I'll hurt you."

Guy with total calm and confidence, declared "There's no way she'd let you."

My response: "Well, he could maim you a little." At that point, they both laughed and Arthur put Guy down. Once again a sense of humor came in handy.

I remained at the L'Enfant Plaza Hotel for three years until Hyatt recruited me to open their 900-room property on Capitol Hill.

The Ritz Carlton - Chicago

In November 1976, The Ritz Carlton in Chicago hired me as their Human Resources Director. I had just finished opening a 900- room Hyatt hotel in Washington, DC. The long hours and the tyrannical general manager influenced my decision to move, as did his constant negative feedback. The new job was better paying and looked to be smart move. With a teenage boy to keep track of, life was stressful and a better salary more than welcome.

The hiring process for the Ritz consisted of a telephone interview with a recruiter and a trip there to meet the general manager. The questions asked were routine and easy to answer. For instance, no one asked me for specifics on my approach to a personnel function or what type of challenges interested me.

They offered me the job on the spot. The salary meant rapid relocation with a major pay increase. On the plane trip back, I debated making the move: It meant selling my house quickly and another change of schools for my son.

Still undecided after an early morning flight back East, I arrived at work by 10 a.m. The General Manager saw me in the lobby and took the opportunity to berate me publicly for being late. In this job, I generally spent six days a week working 10-12 hectic hours in a day. His nastiness clinched my decision. I gave him my notice that day later in the afternoon.

I found a smart real estate agent, who inspected my tidy 3-story attached townhouse and only made one decorating suggestion: The dining room needed a good rug to hide the marred floor. With an American Express card filling in for my lack of cash, I shopped at Sloane's. I found and bought a beautiful oriental rug, well beyond my means. The hope was that the house would sell before the bill came in. It did. A substantial offer came with the first Open House and the profit margin surprised me. We closed, packed up, and left within the month.

At first, living in Chicago, working hard and knowing no one was difficult. However, the new job presented fascinating challenges. The bigger salary meant that for the first time since my divorce, child support was not needed.

I enrolled Guy in the nearest Catholic High School. Then, since everyone warned me about Chicago winters, I walked the neighborhood of Water Tower Place until I found a roomy two-bedroom apartment. No more worry about driving in the snow or having a hard time getting to work. The apartment was a half block away from the employees' entrance to the hotel. Just perfect. Guy's school was a five-block walk.

This hotel had been open less than a year. They hired me because they "needed to cut turnover and establish better departmental communications." I had no idea of the extent of the existing problems.

The first week there, I received a three-page memo from the general manager, describing the turnover problem. It was poorly worded and did not focus on the issues or possible solutions. My experience included opening several hotels, without experiencing massive turnover. I began to solicit opinions and ideas from my staff and the various department heads.

Hotels are usually divided into 5 major departments that report to the general manager: Rooms, Food and Beverage, Sales and Marketing, Finance and Human Resources.

Within the first few days, my in-box filled up with security reports indicating room thefts. The reports all pointed at "inside jobs." My first thought was to look at the housekeeping staff files. That group has keys and easy access to rooms. When I opened the files, I saw no checked references.

I called my staff of four into a short meeting.

"How come no references exist for the housekeeping staff?"

My assistant said: "Why would we check their references, they're just maids and housemen?"

"Because they have keys to all the guest rooms."

Startled looks. "Oh," said my secretary.

"Oh," said my assistant. The others kept quiet.

To my secretary I said: "Okay, do me a favor and ask the union business agent, Roy Smith to come in to see me."

He stopped by one afternoon and we discussed the issue.

"I'm going to check the references of every housekeeper and fire anyone who has lied. I need your support. However, you can argue with me openly so that the rank and file won't lose confidence in you. What do you think?"

Roy surprised me. "It sounds like a decent plan. You can't keep a dishonest staff. The hotel will never survive."

Then he brought up the issue of unpaid dues. "The Union has received nothing since the Agreement was signed several months ago. I'm assuming the paymaster deducted the dues from the membership."

I looked into it immediately. By studying the payroll run off, I saw two things: there were 1003 people on the payroll and yes, dues had been deducted from the union staff. My eyes told me that there were not 1003 employees working in the hotel. They could be part timers or just not terminated from the system. It proved to be the latter.

I approached the Paymaster and asked her why no money had been sent to the Union. She didn't know.

"When you reconcile the payroll, what account is that money assigned to?"

Her answer: "What does reconcile mean?"

Stunned, I decided to talk to the Controller. It was about two in the afternoon, and I found him in his office. He seemed a bit sleepy and uninterested in the issue. I let him know we would need about $28,000 sent to the local Union. He nodded and said he'd get back to me. My intent had been to alert him, gather information, present a formal check request with back up and then issue a check to the Union.

Before the end of the day, the check was on my desk. I had never worked anywhere where a check was issued with no supporting information, such as request forms signed and approved. No such policies or procedures were in place. I also had no way of knowing if $28,000 was the exact amount needed without scanning several months of payroll information.

Then I began to realize that no unemployment taxes had been deducted. I became aware of this when unemployment claims were denied, as no account had been set up.

In January 1977, Arthur Anderson and Company came into the hotel to audit the first year of operation. At that point, I knew that numerous financial issues needed to be investigated. When the Auditor informed me one day, "You know more about accounting than anyone in that department," I was aghast.

Everywhere I had previously worked, the accounting departments were excellent and the controllers educated me on a regular basis. Opening hotels is not complicated but as one controller taught me, "To open you need a good accountant and an excellent HR department." What had happened to the Ritz? Their opening Human Resources Director was from the military with no hotel contacts or background. He hired a controller with a drinking problem. Often in opening there is no time to check references.

Especially for key managers, it is imperative to find the strongest candidates and verify their abilities carefully. Usually this is done informally through past associates and general knowledge. One thing I also learned about openings, was to hire strong, experienced people in key areas and to never promote anyone into a new title and position at that time. Particularly, in Human Resources, a hotel professional is imperative at the start.

Because of the numerous problems, I decided to call some of my old bosses and search for another job. Most of the turnover was due strictly to poor managers and a faulty selection process. I started to install procedures in the personnel office that insured references were checked. Also, working with my excellent training director, we created and taught interviewing and supervision skills to the department managers.

I saw that the salary structure didn't make any sense: Certain jobs paid more in different departments, when the requirements were basically the same. The executive payroll was paid two weeks in advance- a very strange practice.

Another example was that the Executive Steward appeared on the hourly and the executive payroll and collected overtime on the hourly. Also, because of my understanding of Spanish, I overheard that some stewards had paid him for their jobs. When I brought this to general manager's attention he said "That's none of your business."

Also, the purchasing agent was related to the purveyor we used most often. The fine dining restaurant had a menu in French with no translations. In ownership meetings with the auditor and the Food and Beverage Director, he said that all hotel profit is generated from his department, not the Rooms Division. Banquets were not making money. "No new hotel does well for the first year, particularly because we have limited space."

From my past experience in hotels, I knew differently. Rooms Division costs can be stable and predictable, but Food and Beverage profit can fluctuate with food prices. Also, one hotel opening in New York City had only 500 square feet of banquet space and turned a profit in a matter of months. Everywhere I looked in this property, I saw inefficiency and duplicity.

Finally, after the outside audit, the ownership group called an impromptu Saturday meeting at nine a.m. one unusually cold Chicago day. Three owner representatives were present. Only one was dressed casually for the freezing temperatures, as was I. The other two and the management team were in suits and ties. There were no other women.

From 9 until 5, the major owner's agent asked numerous questions of each manager. A simple lunch was sent in around 1 p.m. I was the last person addressed.

"Mrs. Sherr do you have anything you'd like to say? "My answers took most of the group by surprise. "I have helped open six hotels in New York City and two in Washington DC and never seen one of them fail or experience 450% turnover in the first year."

I explained where I thought the problems existed and suggested that a look at policies and procedures would be a good idea. The principal owner's representative thanked me and closed the meeting.

As I was walking to the elevator the general manager took me aside and said: "Of course, you understand you will no longer be employed here."

"I do, and will resign shortly." I headed to my office to type up my resignation.

The owner's representative who led the meeting appeared within the hour. "You are not to resign. I'll explain to you on Monday. "

On Monday, the general manager was replaced by that owner's representative, Mr. Frommer, who took over the hotel's management. He asked me to continue in my job and to cooperate with a new controller, Jeff Fitzwilliam, joining the group. He was young and smart. I suggested he needed to replace certain people and introduce simple procedures.

Jeff listened but his skepticism was apparent. Many issues were brought to light. Accounts Receivable were extremely high - it seemed sending out bills was not a big priority. The payroll issues were addressed. We executives would be paid after we worked two weeks, not before. The Executive Steward was removed from the hourly payroll and left shortly thereafter.

The food and beverage director was not happy with me and on one occasion he wanted to pay our executive chef an extra two weeks' pay, instead of him taking a vacation. Mr. Frommer called me: "Mr. B. is here and wants to pay the Chef two weeks' pay instead of granting him leave. What do you think?"

"It means that the Chef will receive 54 weeks-of-pay in this year, which is considered bad business practice."

My acting boss said: "Is there any other reason I can't do it?"

"You're the boss and you can do whatever you like. I think it's a bad idea, but I am not the one to approve it, you are. You asked for my opinion and that's it."

This turned out to be a wonderful experience and ultimately led to several years working with Four Seasons Hotels in Washington, DC, and Houston, and San Antonio, Texas.

Heel Caesar

Transplanting my son Guy to Chicago in his sophomore year of high school, found me eager to find the perfect gift for his 16th birthday. He asked for a dog. In fact, he wanted a Newfoundland: a huge breed with a gentle disposition. Ahead of time, the size of the dog bothered me. I told Guy if he could find an AKC registered Newfie, perfectly trained, that would be fine.

I underestimated Guy's level of concentration when motivated. He found himself a handsome dog, 5 years old, well trained and a sweetheart. I met and talked to his owner who assured me if anything happened and the dog was unhappy, she would take him back. I paid her $100.00 and we took him home.

Caesar responsiveness to command impressed us, but I did not have enough strength to grab his attention. Guy took over that job. Caesar seemed happy with us and we loved him at first sight. He was a welcome addition to our life, regardless of his size. Problems came up from outside sources.

When we went into the elevator and anyone entered, Caesar barked them out the door. He was indeed sweet but extremely protective. He would sit next to me and occasionally put a heavy paw or his massive head on my leg when he wanted attention: an affectionate nature looking for love from Guy and me. His company delighted us.

After a week, the building manager came to tell me that Caesar would have to go. She let me know that when we were out of the apartment, his barks "made the whole building shake." An exaggeration but I believed a bona fide complaint on behalf of the other tenants. I asked for time to solve the problem and in the meantime, took the dog to work with me.

I smuggled Caesar into the back door of the Ritz Carlton where I worked. I hid my quiet giant under my big desk in my big office. My staff cooperated and set up interviews in the training room, to prevent any mayhem.

I contacted the previous owner but she refused to take him back. Given the dog's good nature, I decided to advertise and find him a good home. I placed an ad as if written by Caesar.

"I am a 150 pound, very well-behaved Newfoundland. I don't eat much, love children and my owner. I have a personality conflict with our landlord. I am free to a good home." I had 60 responses.

I read the letters and phoned several people to evaluate possibilities. I chose to interview three families in their homes. I decided on a young couple with two small children who had recently lost their German Shepherd to illness. The father was a policeman and his young wife stayed home all day with two children smaller than Caesar.

They were perfect: they loved Caesar and he loved them back. I left the dog in their hands and called every week for a month to be sure all was well.

Lesson learned. That was the last time I ever paid for a pet. I now go to and support Animal Rescue groups.

The Four Seasons Experience

The management of the Ritz Carlton, Chicago was handed over to Four Seasons Hotels, Ltd. in October, 1977. The new general manager, John Sharpe arrived: a Cornell graduate, young, and brilliant. In the first few days he called each management team member into his office for a one-on-one conversation. He wanted to hear our opinions.

I did not hesitate. "If you fired every member of the Management Committee, including me, you would not be making a mistake."

Mr. Sharpe made no comment to that except that "the company doesn't do business that way. "Then he asked me why I made so much money, when I didn't even do payroll. He was accustomed to a Personnel Office being an administrative operation reporting usually to the Controller.

I explained that my value could be in dealing with the unions, the employees and cutting turnover, which is extremely expensive in the long run. At the end of the discussion, he let me know that he was removing me from the management committee. This upset me enough that I contacted my past bosses at Loews Hotels. They were ready to take me back to open a hotel in Texas, but not immediately.

I continued working to improve conditions where possible, while waiting for that job offer.

With the owner representatives, I had been working on correcting major problems. We resolved payroll issues and established the unemployment account demanded by federal and state law.

When Four Seasons' controller, Tony McDade appeared on the scene, progress happened rapidly. We easily worked together to replace unqualified accounting personnel. We identified excess payment to the Union Pension fund and recovered thousands of dollars.

With my Training Manager, we created and taught sessions in Guest Services, Labor Relations, Progressive Discipline, Interviewing, Time Management, and Train the Trainer. My staff, and every department head and manager, attended these classes and turnover slowed down.

My secretary was a bit unhappy with our new directives but when I explained what a solid personnel operation looked like, she and my staff responded. Their mission was to see that employee records were accessible and filed properly. Evaluation and referral of qualified candidates was our job. The department began to run smoothly.

I convinced John Sharpe to meet alone with an hourly representative from every department. He thought they would just gripe. I didn't think so and agreed to go with him. The meeting succeeded. Sharpe understood the issues and began confronting department heads, pushing for change, which indeed occurred.

The staff trusted me and gave me inside information which I conveyed to my boss. Once he asked exactly WHO talked to me and I refused to tell him. "They won't talk to me any more once they become identified," I said.

John Sharpe was easy to work for because he listened carefully, considered the information and if he didn't agree with me, explained why. I was able to change some of his perceptions and he, some of mine. After several weeks, he restored me to the management team when he realized that my mission was to serve the best interests of the hotel. He cared about the staff's welfare which also made my life easier.

When I heard that Four Seasons was planning a hotel opening in Washington, DC, I asked to be hired as their opening Human Resources Director. After an interview with that general manager, he offered me the job and I found my replacement, Debbie Brown. She was young with plenty of energy and brains. She is still with the company as a Vice President in Human Resources.

In 1978, I left the Ritz and headed back East to open a Four Seasons Hotel in Washington, D.C.

Finding the Best

The challenge of my job in Chicago at the Ritz was to find skilled people first, in accounting and as we went along, in every department. Our managers also received training in supervisory skills.

My recruiting success came from talking to capable and smart people in the industry.

"Tell me about the best people you have worked with, what made them valuable, and how can I reach them?"

I am a good listener and able to talk to almost anyone. We needed expert, dedicated people in accounting. One of my contacts told me about a woman in Texas working for Hyatt. I called her. She had a background in payroll, receivables and a reputation for excellence. The controller I worked with at the Hyatt DC verified that assessment and relayed the information to me.

I needed her in Chicago. She came to the interview dressed in a pink polyester pant suit covering a very plump body. She was a true Texan, outspoken with a twang, and smart. As we talked, I realized how bright she was. Since first impressions are important, we went shopping that day for a navy-blue pant suit. The pink polyester would not make it in Chicago - navy blue would.

She passed the interview easily and was hired. I worked side-by-side with her, essentially as her clerk. Little by little we reclaimed more than $100,000 in overpaid pension funds.

She was knowledgeable and efficient with anything she touched. Four Seasons eventually promoted her to a controller position.

A wardrobe change can be life altering.

Traveling To Egypt with Three Teenage Boys

This job as the Human Resources Director at the Ritz, moved me from Maryland to Chicago in 1976. It came with major challenges. To remedy the problems needed all my attention and energy. Then my darling aunt died a year later and left me a bit of money. I decided to spend Christmas 1977 with my brother in Cairo, Egypt.

I invited his son, my nephew Arthur, to join us. Then a friend asked me to take her son as well. Booking tickets on Olympic Airways to leave two days before Christmas may have been a mistake. All went well until the airline went on strike mid- air between Chicago and New York where Arthur waited for us.

Finding other reservations to Cairo became a nightmare, made more difficult during the Christmas holiday. If the boys had been older, splitting them up would have been an option. As the two youngest were 16 and Arthur was 20, they were not going anywhere without me.

I finally arranged new reservations, but there was no way during the holidays to contact my brother and let him know our change in plans.

We made it to Athens but then had a hard time booking a flight to Cairo for all of us. Finally, in desperation, I asked a young bespectacled TWA agent to help me:

"Sir: I need space for my three teenage sons and me on a flight to Cairo. There is no way I can split them up." It was easy to look harried and distraught. I plunked down our passports.

"Madam: These three passports, have three different last names. These are your sons?"

I shrugged. "Three different husbands!"

His expression changed. He looked startled, gulped, turned away a moment and quickly arranged the flight. I still wonder what he thought.

We finally arrived in the Cairo Airport in the dead of night. Because of the mid-east tensions of that era, heavily armed guards stood everywhere. Tired and emboldened, I went over to one who looked like a nice guy.

"I need to telephone my brother in Dokki. Can you help me?" I repeated this in French and Italian

He smiled, put his machine gun down on his chair and in English said: "Come with me, Madam." He brought me to a nearby phone, and dialed the number very slowly. I learned later that this was the only way you could hope for a connection.

I told my brother we would find a cab and be there "whenever". It was well past midnight.

We headed to the suburb of Dokki and arrived in front of a high-walled villa with huge oak doors reminiscent of every gothic novel I ever read. Two tall, elegant young black men, dressed in long Egyptian robes opened the doors before I even knocked. They embraced me. "Oh, Miss Patricia, we are so glad to see you. We have met every plane for two days. Welcome."

My brother, Arthur and his friends followed close behind. We stayed up all night and spent the next few hours, sipping wine, opening presents and thoroughly enjoying our belated holiday.

Our Christmas holiday finally began.

Life in Vienna Virginia

In 1978, Four Seasons transferred me from Chicago to Washington, D.C. to open their newest hotel.

I wanted to return to the East Coast and easily found a small affordable house in Vienna, Virginia. Both Guy and my nephew Arthur wanted to live in the country. This house had an acre of ground and "they would do all the work." I had one month of vacation before the new position began. A friend working in The Hague invited me to spend time with him in Germany. It would be one month to do nothing but read and rest. I took him up on it.

The boys were now 17 and 21 years old and adult enough to be alone a few weeks. Before leaving my new home shared with my favorite teenagers, I filled the kitchen with food and asked a friend to check in on them in case any emergencies came up. They could easily reach me if needed.

My friend worked during the week and on weekends we travelled through Germany- a perfect vacation. When time came to leave, I looked forward to seeing Guy and Arthur and returning to work.

Before boarding the plane, I contacted them and arranged for them to pick me up at Dulles Airport near our house. I knew it would be a long tiring flight.

When I arrived in Washington, the boys were not there. Annoyed I found a cab and headed to my home in Vienna. They were not there either and the car was gone. Now angry, I really blew up when I entered the back door entrance. In front of me was a line of large black garbage bags full to their brims.

Next I went into the kitchen and saw that all the cabinets were open and totally empty. Next the dining room added to my fury. There were tiny dead field mice laying around. The cat, Cisco entered the room with a tiny struggling little critter in his mouth. I picked up cat and mouse, went to the back door and shook Cisco until his prey ran free.

At that point, the car came in the driveway. You could hear me yelling at these two guys, probably as far as the airport. At least, they had the grace to look chagrined. With a barrage of orders from me, they began to clean up. The process took several hours.

When I finally calmed down and asked: "What were you thinking? Why didn't you come and pick me up?"

They told me that they had a big fight that delayed them.

"We couldn't decide which would make you the angrier, not being picked up or the mess in the house." Their unresolved dispute had obviously created my anger.

My advice to them: "Next time pick a choice and go with it."

Aging – Pros and Cons

Some thoughts on dealing with aging besides dwelling on the old saw "Growing Old Ain't for Sissies." People of my generation often say this. They quote Bette Davis and others. The legend is, it was first said by Tommy Corcoran, a politician from the Roosevelt era.

As I've aged, it is clear that though I'm pretty active my body aches all the time. It never did that before. I now have age spots...never had them before. One good thing is I'm not hippy and overweight. That is remarkable since I was destined to be fat according to my brothers and ex-husband.

In high school and later I was pudgy and plump. One year thin, one-year medium and one-year fat. I yo-yo dieted over the years and kept flexible wardrobes.

Several years ago when my knees hurt constantly, my doctor suggested replacement or the option of losing twenty pounds. Surgery did not appeal to me so I went back to Weight Watchers. I'm not sure how many times in my life I have started with them and never finished. All I know is, that the first time there, I was in my twenties. (A LONG time ago!)

A few years ago, I finished the course and am now a lifetime member. None of the weight has come back and I am thinner than my high school days.

My tastes have changed drastically. I find little interest in the Style section of any newspaper. All the young performers look the same and I find the popular music of the day just dreadful.

I don't go the movies on a regular basis because there are no awesome stars anymore. Cary Grant, Spencer Tracy, Marlon Brando were compelling figures on screen. Who of the younger generation of movie idols can match that kind of charisma?

I love that my efficient tax accountant, a woman of my age, amazes me. It's fun to visit her. Her wardrobe is as colorful as the eye glasses that match her outfits. She wears heels, which I have given up in pursuit of balance. She doesn't seem to mind tottering about. I do.

After a long career in Human Resources, my volunteer efforts working with a diverse population seeking jobs, has been fascinating. For more than 10 years, I have worked pro bono with Jubilee Jobs in Washington, DC. For thirty plus years, this group has helped people find employment. The organization serves those who simply lack training or self-confidence, others who may be adjusting to life outside of prison, or have struggled with drug or alcohol abuse, or are immigrants learning to adapt to a new country. I lead interviewing and conflict resolution workshops, write resumes and search for prospective employers for our clients.

Also after dropping out of college years ago, I finally finished a BA degree in 2015 and will probably pursue a Masters. Career coaching, writing, recruiting and studying give me a sense of purpose. I exercise at least 30 minutes a day without going to a gym - the microwave times my effort in short increments. Walking everywhere is another part of my home-grown fitness program.

My social life is rich. I have always valued friendship and know the part it has played in keeping me going when hard times came my way. My friendships are inclusive to say the least. (Old, young, men, women, all races and religions–I even know one die hard Republican!)

What do I miss? I am not sure because adapting to change keeps me pretty busy and occupied.

May I suggest to anyone with too much free time – volunteer in your community. It will expand your horizons and give you a sense of purpose.

Life is a gift to be enjoyed when and while you can.

Acknowledgements

This memoir would not exist if not for the assistance and insistence of two people.

Gloria Blazsik
Guy Sherr

I love, thank and appreciate both of them for their editorial skills and simply believing in me.

Made in the USA
Middletown, DE
17 January 2020

83313226R00078